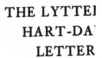

THE LYTTEI
HART-DA
LETTER

THE LYTTELTON HART-DAVIS LETTERS

Correspondence of George Lyttelton
and Rupert Hart-Davis
Volume Three 1958

Edited and introduced by
RUPERT HART-DAVIS

Indulging myself in the freedom
of epistolary intercourse,
I beg leave to throw out my thoughts,
and express my feelings,
just as they arise in my mind,
with very little attention to formal method.

BURKE

JOHN MURRAY

Lyttelton letters
© 1981 Humphrey Lyttelton
Hart-Davis letters and notes
© 1981 Sir Rupert Hart-Davis

First published 1981 by
John Murray (Publishers) Ltd
50 Albemarle Street, London WIX 4BD.
All rights reserved.
Unauthorised duplication contravenes applicable laws
Printed in Great Britain by
Mackays of Chatham

British Library Cataloguing in Publication Data
Lyttelton, George
The Lyttelton Hart-Davis letters.
Vol. 3: 1958
1. English letters
I. Title II. Hart-Davis, *Sir* Rupert
826'.9'1408   PR1347
ISBN 0 7195 3770 3

INTRODUCTION

I am happy to report that the second volume of this correspondence was sufficiently approved to justify the publication of another year's worth. Indeed most readers thought it better than its predecessor because I had removed most of the mutual admiration and drastically restricted the space devoted to cricket and Eton. I have applied the same treatment to this volume.

As before, in the first letters I have retained the opening and signature, which are afterwards omitted, since they are almost always the same: any variation is printed. Similarly I have given our full home addresses in the first two letters and then abbreviated them. From Monday to Friday I lived in a flat above my publishing office at 36 Soho Square. To avoid an excess of footnotes identifying minor characters, most of such names and nicknames will now be found briefly identified in the index.

For beginners I should perhaps add that in 1926 I had been taught by George at Eton, where he was an outstanding teacher and housemaster. He taught mostly classics but in my last year he had started an English course, and it was then that I fell under the spell of his infectious enthusiasm for literature. After I left Eton our ways parted. George taught for a further twenty years before retiring to Suffolk. We met again in 1949 and thereafter saw and wrote to each other occasionally, but the origin of this correspondence was a dinner-party in 1955 during which George complained that no one wrote to him in Suffolk and I accepted his challenge. At the beginning of this volume George was almost seventy-four and I was fifty.

RUPERT HART-DAVIS

Marske-in-Swaledale
November 1980

*This volume is dedicated
by its grateful editor
to his old and dear friends*
DIANA *and* JOCK MURRAY

4 January 1958

My dear George

Many happy returns of the day. I have, alas, no gift to send you—only affectionate good wishes—but I will at least try to post this tomorrow, so that it reaches you on your birthday.

Many thanks for yours from Eton and Cambridge. Has the famous hat reached you safely? Mr Pooter is indeed a new rôle for you, but Adam[1] was certainly unaware of it, since after your departure he expressed his delight in and approval of your coming—a rare tribute from a fourteen-year-old who normally takes everything—including his parents' friends—for granted.

Captain Starlight's horse certainly figured in the film,[2] but anonymously. I too was a fanatical *Black Beauty* fan in early youth, and can still remember—or rather re-experience—my thrills of pity and terror when the stables caught fire.

Last week began with four nights-out running. On Monday I dined quietly with friends in Regent's Park but didn't get home till midnight. On Tuesday I was taken (for the second time, after almost a year) to the two-man review *At The Drop of a Hat*, which I enjoyed all over again. They mostly use the same material, but include one or two topical songs: I rather liked this one of four lines:

> Russia is red, dilly, dilly,
> England is green.
> They've got the Moon, dilly, dilly,
> We've got the Queen.

Afterwards I had to put in an appearance at a New Year's Eve party in Chelsea, but managed to escape before the chimes rang out. Next day I travelled to Brighton in the afternoon, stayed with some friends, and after supper addressed the Hove Quill Club on Oscar

[1] My younger son.
[2] Of *Robbery Under Arms* by Rolf Boldrewood.

Wilde's Letters. Some thirty stalwarts turned up, including (rather disconcertingly) a little girl of nine! Also a fine-looking old boy called E.H. Visiak, an amateur scholar of means who lived with his mother till she died in her late nineties: he edited the Nonesuch Press *Milton* —whether ill or well I know not. Also present was an elderly, amiable and shaggy Oxford don called J.B. Leishman, who has translated most of Rilke's poems into English. I had prepared nothing, but simply let loose on them a hurricane of words, facts and quotations which kept going for three quarters of an hour. They seemed satisfied, even pleased, and we adjourned for some (by me) much needed drinks. Then came a brief visit to some other friends of mine who live nearby, and I got to sleep by one a.m. Next morning I caught an 8.30 train and reached the office just in time to give our assembled travellers a two-hour exhortation on the Spring Books. Lunch with an old friend up from the country, and in the evening *five* hours on the proofs of Diana Cooper's book. To-day we (the family) all drove, mostly through fog, to Moreton-in-Marsh to lunch with Comfort's stepmother. Phew —what a week! And what a lot of licences seem to need renewing— thank heaven we have no dogs, menservants or crests on our carriages!

Sunday morning

I slept for *eleven* hours! and am still so drenched with sleep that there is no sense in me. Adam has volunteered to bicycle to the post office with this, so I must hasten, lest his ardour cool. Needless to say, neither the car's 'log-book' nor the insurance certificate can be found. Duff may know where they are, but he is construing Demosthenes in the drawing-room and I am loth to disturb such unaccustomed assiduity.

The total absence of domestic help is going to produce an intolerable situation when Comfort starts teaching again in a fortnight's time, and I simply don't know what to do about it. There must be people who would be pleased to live here for nothing in return for doing a little housework—for instance a young woman writing a book, and God knows there are plenty of *them*! Perhaps an advertisement in the *New Statesman*? Forgive this drooling: I'm still half-asleep.

Yours ever
Rupert

8 January 1958

My dear Rupert

Your Adam is a good lad—just the sort of look about him that a housemaster likes to see coming into his house—and however stupid housemasters are, they do get rather good at looks, though of course a good many thirteen-year-olds' faces are so to speak neutral. What do you think could have been noticed in George Moore's face at that age? Mere blancmange!

I look forward to meeting T.S. Eliot. Shall I ask Sir Malcolm Sargent if he knows he is known in the music world as 'Flash Harry'? Perhaps not—they are a jealous and backbiting lot, and anyway they can't deny that his tailcoat is the best-fitting in all London. Henry Wood's was a mere bag of ferrets in comparison. I shall see you beforehand and go through my usual hoop of ringing all bells and banging all knockers except the right ones at about 6 p.m. With my new pocket-diary I shall get all 1958 dates right.

Even you must have found that week tiring, but you would, I know, greet any advice to go slower with the same contempt as Johnson, full of dropsy and melancholia and asthma, felt for the Frenchman who said '*Ah, Monsieur, vous étudiez trop*'.

I like that absurd little quatrain. Why is the addition of 'dilly, dilly' so effective? It reminds me of an epitaph told us by my father sixty-five years ago. Have you ever heard it? It is frightfully silly:

'When I am dead, diddle, diddle, (or if you prefer it 'dilly, dilly')
As it may hap,
Bury my head, diddle, diddle,
Under a tap.'
'Under a tap, diddle, diddle!
Pray tell me why.'
'That I may drink, diddle, diddle,
When I am dry.'

It is better than anything in Ezra Pound.

3

I should like to have heard you on O. Wilde, unprepared, all bubbling out of you, fresh and inexhaustible. It was always said that the time to sit listening to Porson[1] was when he was quite sozzled and went on hour by hour 'hicupping Greek like a helot'. Only in one particular is the parallel inexact. I bet it was immensely worth hearing.

I greatly enjoyed Harold Nicolson's book.[2] Why do some call him conceited? It is the book of a particularly likeable and *un*conceited man, don't you agree? I have just begun Jonah's book[3], reading very slowly, as an epicure deals with his cutlets, 'soubees' and cheese 'remmykin'. His writing is full of delicate flavours, as always, and anyone who appears in his pages is most clearly and pleasantly drawn. But I remember some curmudgeonly reviewer saying of his previous book 'Do we want to hear about Balliol characters of half-a-century ago?' A typically *saugrenu* question of course, but won't they be saying it again of the world of Jonah's prime? Among all your publishing confrères you stand out as the one who first of all publishes a book because it is good and not because it will pay. And I am glad to see that in nearly all reviews of your books the external attractiveness is mentioned; they really are beautifully got up.

We are both sympathetic to the verge of distress about your domestic predicament. Perfectly and flawlessly damnable! Advertise wildly and widely. As you say, there *must* be someone somewhere who would gladly come. It is these puttering squalid harassments that get one down. We really long to hear that the situation is saved. And in all this pudder you fill your day, and write to me, and send on my loathsome hat (a million thanks to you both) and are charming to everyone and run the Library and the Lit. Soc. The truth must be frankly faced (*not* 'up to') that you are an exceptionally good man!

Yours ever

G.W.L.

15 January 1958   *Grundisburgh*

Damn that germ![4] We all missed you very much. There was a fine

[1] Richard Porson (1759–1808), Regius Professor of Greek at Cambridge.
[2] *Journey to Java* (1957).
[3] *Georgian Afternoon* by L.E. Jones (1958).
[4] I was in bed with influenza.

gathering, the new ones (to me) being T.S. Eliot, Sir Malcolm and Pryce-Jones. I had luck, being—without any design—between T.S.E. and Sir M. and opposite P.-J. My two neighbours were most friendly and excellent company. I had a good chuckle with T.S.E. A very good man, I thought, with no affectations etc at all. Flash Harry too I liked; he looks extraordinarily young and fresh, which perhaps is not surprising as he said he *enjoyed* (like another I know?) being at work twenty-five hours in the day.

And I was delighted to meet P.-J. again—first time since he was up to me! I was glad to find he is adamant about anonymity in the *T.L.S.*—just as adamant as he was in the most benign manner about the plethora of foreign writers given all that space in his columns.

The *only* snag in these delightful evenings is that one wants to have a crack with practically everybody there. I got hardly a word with Roger, or Peter F. or Bernard F. or Somervell. *Embarras de richesses* with a vengeance. Roger has discovered an occasion in the annals when Spencer Lyttelton and Lord Curzon were the only attendants. Very embarrassing for old Uncle S., who hated a tête-à-tête. He was a superbly handsome and vigorous man, but, well, when E.F. Benson asked him if he had ever kissed a girl, his answer was 'Once—on the brow'. A Victorian old bachelor but somehow not at all spinsterish.

I get this off at once, more than suspecting that, whatever your temperature, you may have written. Please get well at once or sooner.

19 January 1958   *Bromsden Farm*

At last I have succeeded in disappointing you—and a good thing too if it brings down to earth your much too flattering estimate of my kindness and capabilities. I did intend to scribble a few lines last week-end, but as I lay sweating with fever, eyes, nose and whole head occluded by a streaming cataract, I found myself unable even to read or to concentrate for more than a minute or two. It was like a wakeful delirium, neither restful nor enjoyable. I was much concerned about the efficient cancellation of all my plans, and only pray that you were warned in time to prevent a fruitless visit to Soho Square. So glad you enjoyed the Lit. Soc. Tom Eliot is a pet, isn't he? So natural, humorous and unpretentious. Flash Harry (though clearly a bounder) is good company occasionally, and very friendly. Did I tell you how once at the beginning of a big dinner-party at Hamish Hamilton's I was approached by a very pretty girl whom I scarcely knew? 'Will you promise me something?' she asked earnestly, out of the blue. 'Anything,' I gallantly replied, strengthened by a powerful Martini. 'Promise me,' she said, 'that whatever happens I shan't have to go home alone in a taxi with Malcolm Sargent.' I duly promised, but later regretted my quixotry, since we had to wait till the small hours before Flash Harry gave up the chase, and then of course I had to escort the lady to South Kensington.

Poor old Jonah, every minor detail concerning his new book (have you read it yet?) has gone wrong. Ages ago we arranged that he should come in shortly before publication (next Friday) and sign some copies for special friends, which I would then send out. He chose to come when I was away: my secretary nursed him with blotting-paper and labels: she assured him the books would not go out for a week, and then went to lunch. When she got back she found that the packer, seeing the books ready and thinking to be helpful, had packed and despatched them all. It didn't matter a jot, but it upset poor Jonah unduly. On Friday I got a charming note from Roger, marked on the envelope 'TO AWAIT RETURN OF STRENGTH', which I rather liked.

Still no sail on the domestic ocean, but various local steps are being taken. Duff is back at Oxford, and Adam returns to Eton on Tuesday, after a day and night in London with Dad: he goes up with me in the morning. I shall give him dinner at the Garrick and take him to a theatre, get his hair cut, and try to buy him some flannel trousers and a tweed jacket. He is as tall as many grown men, but has no hips or shoulders to speak of.

I have, as you can imagine, little news to recount, save incoherent sickroom musings. Next Wednesday I am to dine with Tommy Lascelles and wife in their grace-and-favour apartments in Kensington Palace, and on Thursday with old Heygate's daughter Liza, an old friend of my sister's and mine. I must redouble my London Library efforts, to make up for lost time, and you've no idea what four days' absence does to my office desk.

I have got Oscar out of prison now, basking in the summer sunshine of Dieppe in the brief lull before the poverty, squalor and degradation of his last three years. The story still has power to move me, and I think will always affect those who are susceptible of being purged by the pity and terror of a man's destiny. When I've finished the annotation (there will be more than a thousand footnotes) I shall rough out a general introduction and brief prefaces for the nine parts into which I have divided the book. *Then* I shall have to read the whole damned thing through again, adding new footnotes, supplying endless cross-references and generally tidying up. Meanwhile new letters still trickle in, and I hope they'll continue to do so until my first proofs have gone back to the printer. When will that be?

23 January 1958   *Grundisburgh*

Shakespearean hunch: I am sure in my own mind that the adjective 'whoreson' came into *his* mind from some experience in Suffolk of a day like 22 January 1958; there is no other completely fitting epithet. I was in Ipswich and at precisely 12.21 midday fell headlong on the pavement—without, I may say, the smallest damage or even discomfort; I might have been a slalom champion in embryo. The only discomfort was caused by two citizens, who thought they were helping me, 'offering unneeded arms, performing dull farces of escort' (do you know those superbly absurd hexameters of Clough's *Bothie*?). To-day the sun is here, but, like Bet Flint vis-à-vis Mrs Williams's disapproval, the frost 'makes itself very easy about that.'[1]

I do hope you are being *immensely* careful not to overdo it after that flu. It is a vindictive germ, and Suffolk is full of men who are nursing cardiac murmurs and upsets of various kinds through resuming hard work too soon. But I suspect you are one of those good men who pay not the smallest attention to such advice—or indeed any.

[1] 'I have known [said Dr Johnson] all the wits from Mrs Montagu to Bet Flint!' 'Bet Flint!' cried Mrs Thrale; 'pray who is she?' 'Oh, a fine character, madam! She was habitually a slut and a drunkard, and occasionally a thief and a harlot ... Mrs Williams,' he added, 'did not love Bet Flint, but Bet Flint made herself very easy about that.' (Fanny Burney's Diary, August 1778).

How right you are about T.S.E. and Flash H. The former said several excellent things, but, as Dr Johnson praised in Beauclerk, without a trace of self-consciousness. And the genially bounding Flash H. I have always heard that his morals were less admirable than e.g. the sit of his tail-coat, which is admirable. Your tale of that girl is very sinister. H.G. Wells was like that—and so was Mr Pepys, whose propensity I have seen mysteriously and unconvincingly ascribed to his stone in the bladder—not that that is more ridiculous than some of the Freudian excuses for criminals. Soon they will be whitewashing Neill Cream,[1] as Graves has Palmer.[2] (Have you read *They Hanged my Saintly Billy*? I haven't.) Or rather he seems to hint that P. was innocent. But Dr Kenealy recorded that P. gave him an impression of absolute evil. Sir Guy Stephenson who married my cousin told me that he and Bodkin (lately dead) both had the same feeling about George Joseph Smith (Brides-in-Bath), almost a sort of lowering of one's temperature, as Utterson (was it?) had in the presence of Mr Hyde. Interesting, if not *ex post facto*.

I have just read Hesketh Pearson's *Gilbert*—a dreadfully tiresome man—huffy and irascible, and at the same time thinking much of his fame, and despising the achievement which created it. Very like Conan Doyle, who thought highly of *A Duet* and scorned Sherlock Holmes. Have you ever read Gilbert's plays? Frightfully feeble and soft and stilted. But the man who could pour out such lines as 'An affection à la Plato for a bashful young potato, or a not-too-French French bean' shall surely remain immortal.

I have also read Sir Russell Brain's *Tea with Walter de la Mare*. Slight but enjoyable, though there is rather too much about the difference between the brain and the mind etc. Did you know him? Manifestly a delightful chap. There is one tremendous gaffe: Brain says that de la Mare thought 'A Mr Wilkinson, a clergyman' was an actual line of Wordsworth's, and then adds that it was invented, as a

---

[1] A bald-headed squinting doctor who was executed in 1892 for murdering a number of women with strychnine.

[2] In 1856 William Palmer, a young surgeon of Rugeley in Staffordshire, was executed for the murder by poison of John Parsons Cook. It is almost certain that he had previously murdered many other people, including his wife, several of his illegitimate children, and his brother.

typically bad W. line, by Flecker!—when in several books on Tennyson and FitzGerald it is recorded that both claimed the authorship. He (R.B.) misquotes 'Golden lads and lasses must' which is of course what Shakespeare ought to have written but—most inaccountably—he wrote 'and girls all must'. Very odd, surely.

And a neighbour has lent Pamela Clare Sheridan's Diary—title forgotten—which with her outlandish experiences strikes me as not quite as good as it ought to be. But surely her heads in plaster or bronze of Lenin, Gandhi, and Winston are fearfully good? All the same one constantly feels a mild wonder that no one has killed her.

Must stop. *Foul* music by Gordon Jacob just over, in which the pianist stamped on, kicked, butted, thumped and finally threw out of window the long-suffering piano. Now *The Unfinished* removes the nasty taste; though George Hurst, the conductor, is taking it as fast as he bowled. I love the way Schubert (like Beethoven) falls in love with his air and simply cannot say goodbye to it. Bless them both—and you too.

26 January 1958   *Bromsden Farm*

As though to herald the cold spell, last week-end some sort of burglar broke into my office (apparently by using builders' ladders from next door) and stole my only warm overcoat. I was too busy to do anything about it till Friday, when the cold drove me to buy a fine new coat, for which I trust the insurance company will pay. If they do I shall be better off than before, since the old coat had weathered twelve winters and was rather tight. Nothing else seems to have been taken, and I can imagine the intruder gnashing his teeth over so many useless books and papers.

I do hope that fall really did you no harm. Large men fall heavily. Please keep away from treacherous ground.

Jonah's book has started off quite well, with a full-page leading review in *Punch*, a fine one in the *Telegraph*, tolerable ones in the Sunday papers and a good recommendation from the Critics on the wireless this morning. The dear old fellow is now deaf even on the telephone, where most deafness seems to disappear.

Russell Brain is a member of the Johnson Club, and a very agreeable fellow (the two statements are not necessarily contradictory). I enjoyed his book very much, because I could recognise old de la Mare's authentic voice in the conversations, and I admired the unpretentiousness of it all.

Last Monday I took Adam up to London, got his hair cut, gave him lunch, and sent him for the afternoon with one of my staff to the Imperial War Museum—Adam's choice and much enjoyed. Then steak and claret at the Garrick and on to *At the Drop of a Hat*. It was my third visit, but I enjoyed it as much as ever, especially since A. adored it. He slept in the flat, and in the morning I bought him a tweed jacket and some flannel trousers, and put him in a taxi to Paddington.

On Wednesday I dined with the Lascelles. They have made a lovely flat out of the old stables of Kensington Palace, quiet and warm and comfortable. Lady L. (daughter of Lord Chelmsford) is charming, and so is their daughter Lavinia, who was there with her husband. Also present were Tony Thesiger and his wife (née Virginia Graham, daughter of Harry G. and a life-long friend of mine), and Mrs Mulholland (née Harcourt) who is just about to take off for the Antipodes with the Queen Mother. All very agreeable and easy.

Next night I dined with Liza Heygate in Chelsea, in company with Hester Chapman (novelist and another old friend), Mr Justice Upjohn and wife (rather disconcertingly called Bubbles), and a middle-aged Jewish pansy from Manchester. Also agreeable, but I must try and keep some evenings for the work which now threatens to overwhelm me. Diana's proofs are uppermost, and it looks as though I shan't get them to press without a visit to Chantilly. I may go on Friday, and return on Sunday, so perhaps you'd better write to Soho Square this week.

In one of his letters to Diana, written from the front in 1918, Duff praises Meredith's 'The Story of Chloe' as one of the best short stories in the language. I read it last night—with some difficulty, since it's almost impossible to see the story for the words, but there is one excellent chapter (where Chloe plans her suicide), and in some way the effect of the whole story is greater in retrospect than at the time. If you've got it, do try it and let me know what you think.

Did you read Alan Moorehead's stuff in to-day's *Sunday Times*?

Jolly good, I thought, though I'm sure that Arthur Ransome, with whom I dine tomorrow, will pick holes in it. He was in Russia from 1913 to 1918, and nobody else is right, bless him—and you.

30 January 1958   *Grundisburgh*

First to make you green with envy (but not, I am confident, with hatred and malice) let me tell you I am writing this in the summer-house. The eye of the sun, I grant you, is hardly more than squinting at me over the wellingtonia, but I can detect a little heat in it, though, like other cynical visitors, I suspect that you might say that most of it is supplied by my imagination. Unlike Bolingbroke I find no difficulty in wallowing naked in December snow by thinking on fantastic summer's heat.[1] But I am not in this respect so offensive as Toddy Vaughan[2] who was popularly supposed not even to possess a great-coat. I say, how sickening about yours and that damned burglar. Mind you press the insurance folk hard; it may be just the sort of claim they like meeting for the advertisement. But they are a little apt to ask tiresome questions as to how old the lost coat was. You must stress the sentimental value of the dear old coat, what superior cloth old coats were made of etc. The builder whose ladder helped the chap ought to have a slightly uneasy conscience, but probably builders don't keep such things.

What has happened to John Heygate? He wrote a worthless much-puffed book about Eton nearly twenty years ago (*Decent Fellows*) and nothing ever again. His father was a colleague for some years—not an unamiable man, and immensely efficient in a philistine way. Mrs H. was a grim sardonic woman who knew all about football and rowing and had a sharp edge to her tongue. I treasure a remark of hers that the only thing Eton boys learnt thoroughly was the one thing Eton masters knew least about, i.e. good manners. Not bad.

Did you know M.D. Hill who died last week—as he told me a fortnight ago he was about to do, quite placidly. What had clearly happened to him is, I suppose, common at eighty-five, i.e. a complete loss of interest in all that is going on—a sort of *uncoupling* of one's mind from world affairs, human interests, old habits etc. He was a

[1] *Richard II*, Act I, Scene 3.   [2] Former Eton master.

blunt, matter-of-fact scientist but, *not* being a Wykehamist, had plenty of humour and could laugh even at himself. I liked him and we corresponded pretty regularly. My chief Eton correspondent is Wilfrid Blunt, who published recently a perfectly delightful book *Persian Spring*—*disgracefully* reviewed, by the way, in the *T.L.S.* Sneering at him as Mr Chips, wrapped up in Eton, prejudiced, intolerant and mocking about oriental ways etc—the truth being *exactly* the opposite of all these sniffy epithets. Do read it; it doesn't take long. It contains one witticism of real brilliance, referring to those old codgers who throng to Henley in July, what he calls the 'Leanderthal' type. And if that isn't of Oscarian vintage—well I ask *you*?

'The Tale of Chloe.' I read it at Cambridge, I think, and had it at Eton, where some boy borrowed and failed to return it. I remember nothing of it—except, wasn't there somebody in it called The Duchess of Dewlap? And in the same volume there was an excellent tale called 'General Ople and Lady Camper' which I remember thinking very funny. Was I right? Will Meredith ever come back? The world his people lived in is so completely dead. But then so is Henry James's and he apparently is reviving, though I don't suppose John Osborne reads him; how could he? There is as far as I recollect *no* allusion to a water-closet in either Meredith or James. Mugwumps! Mandarins! Stuffies! What can such old mokes know about *LIFE*?

I hope you are *quite* restored to health? You don't say a word about it. My fall left no ill effects, though 'between the stirrup and the ground,' so to speak, I remembered Amsler's[1] saying that a very large percentage of big men over seventy died from the effects of a fall. But not yet!

I must stop—having a slight but persistent feeling that my letters are getting too long, just as I have an equally persistent but far from slight conviction that I talk too much. Like Gilbert, who was disconcerted by the unexpectedly loud laughter when he jokingly said some people thought him quarrelsome. I see grins all round the table when I say I talk too much, hoping to be contradicted.

P.S. When Heygate's won the football cup, the players were presented by Mrs H. with Bibles bound in the house-colours (blue and yellow).

[1] Eton doctor.

Writing in your summer-house in January! Please go indoors at once, and try no more alfresco composition until the swallow dares. We have aconites and many snowdrops in flower: can spring be far behind? Yes, it bloody well can, as we shall doubtless see.

The insurance company has paid the whole cost of my new overcoat, and I remember how old publishers used to pray for 'a fire at the binder's', which would turn their unsaleable stock into much-needed cash. Did you read the article on Publishing in yesterday's *Times*? I think I told you they asked me to write it, and I'm doubly glad I didn't, since I couldn't possibly have mentioned my own name. I thought it quite good and pretty accurate, though, as they say, 'slanted' from the point of view of the big battalions. I must discover who wrote it.

I'm delighted to tell you that *Georgian Afternoon* is booming. We sold 550 copies last week (its first), and the booksellers had first to get rid of their pre-publication orders. Jonah is in high fettle, delighted with all his reviews and letters, and markedly less deaf! One of the places I saw him was at Ursula Ridley's. When I arrived, there were five women (very charming ones) and no men. I drank a whisky-and-water briskly, and when Ursie said 'Help yourself to another', I poured out a stiff whisky and filled up the tumbler with what I thought was iced water but turned out to be strongish Martini! Ursie wanted to throw it away, but I insisted on drinking it, and I can now tell you that a tumbler of Martini containing a large whisky is a great tongue-loosener. I held the five women in thrall, and when Jonah and Evy arrived they must have wondered at my eloquence. Later this same drink, backed up by a glass or two of this and that, sustained me through dinner at White's with my father and the Duke of Argyll. The Duke is dullish and rather pompous, but in my ultra-uninhibited mood I remembered that he spent years trying to fish up a Spanish treasure-ship from the sands of Tobermory Bay, and so encouraged him to describe the whole enterprise.

John Heygate has retired to Ireland, where he very happily does nothing with his third wife and some assorted children. He is amiable but irredeemably silly.

I was sad to read of Piggy Hill's death, and of Lubbock's. I was up to both of them, though, as I have often told you, the only beaks who inspired me were you and Wickham. The others were nicer or nastier, cleverer or stupider, but *not* inspiring.

I think that the 'uncoupling' of the mind at eighty-five, such as you describe in Piggy Hill, might well be a blessed state, though eighty-five needn't be the age for it.

Next Friday at 10 am I leave Victoria in first-class comfort, looking forward to a superb lunch on the French train. Diana will meet me in Paris and drive me out to Chantilly. Saturday will be devoted to the proofs of her book, and on Sunday morning I return by the same route. Write to Soho Square and I'll scribble an answer in the train. Shall I send it to Grundisburgh? When do you come to London? I shall expect you at 6 on the Tuesday—what fun!

I can't remember whether you've read Faber's *Jowett*—forgive my stupidity. I've just got down to it and am enjoying it enormously. The opening chapters are beautifully written, and I don't mind G.F's occasional thrusting in of himself (a habit in biographers which usually maddens and disgusts me).

Adam is up to Bobby Bourne and says he is 'v. nice'. Duff looked in for lunch from Oxford: he is still finding Greats tiresome after his military and other excursions, and I dare say a year of Oxford is all he will take.

I have just listened to Bertrand Russell propounding a new theory of the universe on the radio, but I had to leave the room in the middle and lost the thread—which I daresay I should have done in any case. Science is a closed book to me, and there are so many others I badly want to open.

5 February 1958   *Grundisburgh* (*summer-house!*)

It is spring-like this morning and, as with you, the garden is dotted with snowdrops 'hailing far summer with uplifted spear'[1] (which I warn you I quote *every* February every bit as unrepentantly). Your comment on Shelley's optimistic query I actually found pencilled

[1] Quotation untrace

14

in the margin of an Ipswich library book some time ago, proving once again that what Suffolk thinks today London does to-morrow.

Very good about your overcoat. Mind you get a really good one, and avoid having flu twice in the winter. Yes, I read that article on publishing with interest, as your name suddenly caught my eye. Did you know old George Longman, an immensely worthy, straitlaced, rather ungenial man? Fifty years ago he said that he always gave the same advice to any young man who thought of going in for publishing, viz 'Don't'. However he wasn't head of the firm, and his second son Bobby (a great friend of mine at Eton and Cambridge and very rarely seen since) did go into the firm and has just retired, not I gather bankrupt, so G's advice looks a little timorous. He was a very good bat in the early 70's. I can remember about ten individual strokes that I saw made since 1897. One of Trumper's in 1905 stands out because it was unique, i.e. in none of the books, and never made before or since. Oddly enough one was a square *cut* by Rhodes, who later forbade the Harrow boys ever to cut (or 'coot') as it was unsafe. ('But, Wilfred, a cut's the greatest fun.' 'Cricket's not meant to be foon'—which ought to be in the *Oxford Book of Quotations*, being on the same level as Goering's 'Guns are better than butter'.)

But I weary you. I imagine the success of Jonah's book will help him with the Lit. Soc. Good! I was immensely tickled by your saying it had diminished his deafness; publishers must see human nature with frightening penetration. Also I enjoyed your rake's progress from Martini to Martini—making glad the heart of both R.H-D. and His Grace of Argyll. Was he at Eton? If so, no doubt called Hamilton. *All* dukes at one time or another seem to be called Hamilton. (It is drenching at the moment, and the rain on my tarred felt roof makes a fine tattoo.)

Jowett: yes, indeed, but surely I told you how much I had enjoyed it and added some probably irrelevant comments about the resemblance between J. and Hitler, i.e. some genital inadequacy or oddity. But I expect it was towards the end of a letter, and very faint and few are those who get as far as that—as Macaulay said of those who were in at the death of the Blatant Beast (which, in cold fact, hasn't happened by the end of *The Faery Queen*. It must have been the only book which Macaulay didn't finish).

15

(The sun is emerging. They that endure to the end shall be saved.)
I look forward as always to next Tuesday. The only members I have
never seen there are E.V. Knox, Balcarres, Laurence Irving and John
Betjeman—excluding some like Harold Caccia in another continent
and of course the P.M. *He* has just left N.Z., and my nephew, the
Governor-General, found him very aloof and inattentive, but charit-
ably supposes he may have been tired. But he does add how disappointing great public men are to meet—as Max Beerbohm once
said, I believe. I haven't met many P.M's or ex-P.M.s. Eden was an
icicle, Attlee amiable but wholly non-committal, Winston as Laski
described him—'like a great actor playing a part'. Baldwin seemed
more human at the top of Lord's pavilion during a Test Match, but he
fell asleep long before any test could be applied. And years ago A.J.B.
shed over all the company streams of that impersonal geniality which
leaves one with the firm conviction that fundamentally he doesn't
care a straw about anyone. Birkenhead was tight the first time I met
him, and showed off interestingly but rather repellently on the second
occasion. Half the present cabinet have or ought to have touched their
hats to me,[1] but that won't save the country, though in a few years'
time it may well be that the country wishes they were back.

9 February 1958   *36 Soho Square*

I meant to write to you on the ship to-day, but I had eaten so
heavily and so well on the French train that when the time came I
spent the brief sea-voyage half-asleep in an armchair. And now I am
sleepy and silly after a long day's journey.

On Friday morning I just had time to look through the post before
catching the ten o'clock train and there was your faithful letter, bless
you. I read it in the icy train. The snow started in mid-Channel, and
my train was three quarters of an hour late in Paris. At Chantilly all
the telephone lines were down—and still are. The only other guest
was Loelia (née Ponsonby), last-but-one Duchess of Westminster.
I spent most of yesterday going through the proofs with Diana. The
house is centrally heated, and one can't get used to that in one day.

[1] As boys at Eton.

Last night Frank Giles, the *Times* Paris correspondent, came to dinner with his wife (a daughter of Lord De la Warr)—nice young gay people. The whole expedition was quite an amusing change, though considerably less restful than my usual week-end.

I shall expect you here about six on Tuesday, to admire the clock *in situ*. Malcolm Sargent is coming again to the Lit. Soc.: you must have charmed him! The election went as I forecast last week, so you will soon be able to test Jonah's hearing. His book is still going well, I'm glad to say.

Forgive this miserable snippet of a letter. Next Sunday I will resume my normal rhythm.

67 Chelsea Square
London S.W.3

13 February 1958

This cannot be more than a scrap designed mainly as a gesture of defiance to the absurd notion that seeing you on Tuesday could be considered a valid reason for not writing to you on Thursday.

The dinner, as always, was immensely repaying. I sat between the same two as I did a year ago on my first appearance when I was most graciously put at my ease by Tommy Lascelles and surely the nicest of all lawyers, Sir D. Somervell.

I told Peter F. of the pleasant article in the February *National Review* by John Verney (signed 'Trix' and with a good deal of reference to 'Strix'[1]) and your penetrating eye will to a great extent gather from it what sort of chap he is (curious how clearly one sees that in many cases but emphatically not in all). Tommy L. was much amused with the additional chit about Charles Morgan in *The Times*, commending him as a conversationalist. We recalled a dinner at which we all were which C.M. nearly killed till (according to T.L.) I, if you please, talked him into silence. The evidence that I am the most garrulous of ancients grows steadily. I must do something about it. Don't be surprised if, when we next meet, all you get from me is a beautiful smile tinged with sadness, and no words at all. Not all that easy, I suspect, and I remember Hensley Henson's summing up of his

[1] Peter Fleming's pseudonym in the *Spectator*.

Dean, Welldon: 'a man who can neither speak with effect, nor be silent with dignity.' What a grandly perceptive eye *he* had—and the crispest possible style. I must stop, but I leave with you, after all this drip, one thing of his which you will appreciate. It hits an old house-tutor full in the wind. His comment on 'that strange institution the public school': 'I cannot think that the conscientious and devoted governess method, sublime in its self-dedication and Pharisaic in its scrupulosity, can be altogether wholesome for the development of character.' Well, there you are; the old brute (whom I love) doesn't attack the system, as do others, at one of its *weak* points, but at what is usually thought its strong point.

Still I did always try to follow that shrewd advice of C.M. Wells to A.B. Ramsay: 'Ram, I'll tell you a thing; don't see *too much* of your chaps.' It is *very* wise. And when one saw boys *drained* of individuality by too conscientious tutoring one realised it to the full.

Perhaps 'scrap' isn't altogether *le mot juste* for this letter. It is *your* fault. I start, and then I see your face and hear your voice, and remember half-a-dozen things you said, and the thoughts (too big a word?) begin to throng. How horribly duller my old age would be if this correspondence had never started!

P.S. Charles Morgan died in his sleep. His wife has just told Diana. They had been discussing the poet Traherne.

16 February 1958   *Bromsden Farm*

Your splendid 'scrap' from Chelsea was awaiting me here on Friday evening. Clearly the motto on the paper, *Ventis Secundis*, must stand for Second Wind. Jonah's joy at *his* election was unbounded and most touching. Directly he got Tommy's letter on Friday morning, he rang up to say it was the nicest thing that had ever happened to him, and he was so very grateful to you and me for putting him up. That same morning Jonah's book was magnificently reviewed all over the centre page of the *T.L.S.*—by Alan P.-J. himself, I feel sure—so the old boy's Valentine was a pretty good one.

Some day you must introduce me to John Verney: Peter told me to-day that he had read that article in the *National Review* and thought it excellent. Have you by any chance got a copy of it to lend me? I much enjoyed Hensley Henson on public schools: did you know him? Is there a good biography? With letters?

I have had a charming letter from Hilda Morgan, Charles's widow. She is naturally distressed by the inadequacy and mediocrity of most of the obituaries. I am telling her not to worry about C's literary reputation, which will inevitably find its own level in the end, and I'm sending her that Emerson passage which I sent you a few weeks ago. I shall go to the memorial service at St Margaret's on Thursday: it starts at noon, and at one I have to take the chair for a bookseller at a lunch-time meeting at the National Book League in Albemarle Street. A fast taxi will be needed, in which I shall reverse my double-sided jersey from black to scarlet, and whip on another tie, so as not to depress the assembled booklovers. There was a splendid row at last week's meeting of the Royal Literary Fund, during which the secretary and the treasurer accused each other of idleness and incompetence. If only all committee meetings were as lively!

This springlike weather is most beguiling. We have snowdrops, scyllas and yellow crocuses in flower, and yesterday I saw a pair of pied wagtails who showed every sign of setting up house. Today we lunched out of doors, and I imagined you in your beloved summer-house.

Since then, apart from an hour's gardening of the rougher kind, I have been reading one manuscript after another, until I never want to see one again—and so many books all round waiting to be read! Also I spent an hour on poor neglected Oscar, whom I have now got to Naples in the autumn of 1897—the beginning of his decline. Although I now know his whole life backwards and forwards (which is often the way I have to work at it) I still feel moved as I retrace every step of his terrible journey. How tickled he would be to know that someone was spending years of patient work on the minutiae of his life's correspondence!

Diana Cooper's first volume is now, thank goodness, passed for press, and soon I shall have to start work on the second volume, which is already in rough typescript, waiting for me to cut it into chapters, correct the spelling, supply punctuation and generally knock it into shape. She is even now starting to write the *third* volume!

Duff writes from Oxford to say that he and a friend are meditating a drive across the Sahara in a Land Rover. I have written back sternly, saying that I have seldom heard of a more pointless idea. What next? My daughter Bridget writes from New York to say that Alistair Cooke thinks he can get her a baby-minding job in Arizona. She, bless her, always manages to pay for herself, and I have encouraged her to go, though it would be nice to have her home for a bit to help with the housework. A London flat, which a daily woman can more-or-less clean in an hour, has its advantages. Can you manhandle a Hoover? Nor can I.

19 February 1958   *Grundisburgh*

The snow is responsible for this beastly Biro, because I ought to be in the summer-house. In the drawing-room I am a sufferer from that strange feminine dislike for a masculine table a-drip with masculine gadgets which must not be touched, so I am condemned to an arm-chair and Biro. I used to employ an ordinary pen and an inkpot (full of midnight-black indelible ink) poised on the arm of the chair. I cannot say it was a popular set-up, and for quite a time could not understand why. But I did in the end. My plea that, on that occasion, the fact that the chair-covers were away at the cleaners showed that the Almighty was on my side was not well received. Hence an occasional spell of this graphological abortion.

I also had a delightful letter from Jonah. Last Friday certainly was a good day for him—though he modestly says P.-J.'s *T.L.S.* review must be discounted as he is a personal friend, and indeed a relative of his wife's. But I saw nothing in the review which could be faulted on this ground, though of course it was conspicuously benevolent—and yet quite different from those too numerous reviewers who nail every other book with words like 'masterpiece', 'genius', 'irresistible' and 'exquisite'. How much, by the way, some of them are irritated by Harold Nicolson. Some by things in his Java book (which I greatly enjoyed) but chiefly, apparently, by his *Observer* reviews. A silly (I know) young (I suspect) man, who calls himself Humphry Clinker, in a paper called *Books and Art*, has an article called 'Nicolson's Disease', which apparently consists in having an urbane and cultured manner. It seemed to me quite toothless, all bark and no bite; and how tired I am of such adolescent wisecracks as saying that H.N.'s writing gives H.C. 'the kind of sensation which might result from the sound of a silver-plated bassoon down which someone had carelessly stuffed one of the late Lord Curzon's socks'. If that isn't damned bad and silly writing, then I must go back to Remove again. I feel, on reading that sort of stuff, exactly as I did when reading *Lucky Jim*, which, alas, Jonah tells me he thought very funny. There is no doubt I am 'unprofitably travelling towards the grave' (is anything much better than a *good* Wordsworth line?).

I tried to get a *National Review* in Ipswich yesterday, but failed—though one bookseller has heard of the thing. I read it—not all through—in the Borough Library. Hasn't your club a copy? But I suspect you have no time to go there. Next to John Verney is an excellent critique by another old pupil John Bayley—now of New College (called by David Cecil his best English pupil some twelve years ago). He seems to me to hit off one or two aspects of Kipling and Conrad very happily.

There is a two-volume biography of Henson (by Braley) and two vols of *Letters* and *More Letters*. You can skip quite a lot in both, for I suspect your appetite for œcumenical affairs of forty years ago is no stronger than mine, but there is plenty besides. Of course you know his episcopal charge on 'Buchmanism'? A superb and shattering description with exactly *one* derogatory adjective and no more. Out of print now, but if you haven't read it do let me lend my copy to you. It won't take an hour to read, but, my hat, you will enjoy it.

Who did the *Times* obituary of Charles Morgan? Because wasn't that rather distinguished? I suppose he was not a man it was easy to feel *warm* affection for. I liked him on the two or three occasions when I met him—also all his *Reflections in a Mirror* and two plays which were really about something. I hope you managed your quick change in the taxi, and had no such contretemps as the absent-minded peer who arrived at the graveside wearing an I.Z.[1] tie.

What a spirited family you have! Of course there is no point in

[1] I Zingari, a cricket club, whose colours are red, yellow and black.

crossing the Sahara in a Land Rover, but how reassuring that there should still be young men who think there is. And a daughter baby-minding in Arizona must cheer the heart of any father except a James Forsyte ('She'll be knocking herself up one of these days, gadding about like that').

Your committee-meetings sound better fun than mine, in which even questions like 'Should there be a lavatory adjoining the school armoury?' raise no real heat in discussion. But at Ipswich the mutual hatred of the HM and the Bursar shows signs of developing on interesting lines. But what petty tiffs we have now compared with e.g. that of old Butler, Headmaster of Shrewsbury, with his Lower Master. For *thirty-six* years they did not speak to each other, and transacted all the school business by letter. And some still regard the Victorians as 'cissy'!

Jonah's happiness continues, for I have ordered a second impression of *Georgian Afternoon*. By the time it arrives in the middle of March the first edition (6000) should be exhausted. (I am exhausted now, but that is habitual, and beside the point.)

I had better leave Hensley Henson for my old age: if only he had flourished *sixty* years ago I could justifiably hunt through him for side-lights on people Wilde knew.

Ploughing through Emerson for that missing quotation I keep coming on copy-worthy bits. Whether you know it or not, here's one:

A foolish consistency is the hobgoblin of little minds, adored by little statesmen and philosophers and divines. With consistency a great soul has simply nothing to do. He may as well concern himself with his shadow on the wall. Out upon your guarded lips! Sew them up with packthread, do. Else, if you would be a man, speak what you think to-day in words as hard as cannon-balls and to-morrow speak what to-morrow thinks in hard words again, though it contradict every thing you said to-day. Ah, then, exclaim the aged ladies, you shall be sure to be misunderstood. Misunderstood!

It is a right fool's word. Is it so bad then to be misunderstood? Pythagoras was misunderstood, and Socrates, and Jesus, and Luther, and Copernicus, and Galileo, and Newton, and every pure and wise spirit that ever took flesh. To be great is to be misunderstood.

One doesn't hear any uncompromising voices like that nowadays, more's the pity. The telling phrase (rhetorical though it may be) looks like dying with Winston. How indomitably that old warrior battles on! Pneumonia and pleurisy at eighty-three can't, even to-day, be negligible complaints. Perhaps pickling in old brandy is the best prophylactic.

Charles Morgan's memorial service was well attended, and the choir (some dozen men) sang beautifully—the closing Nunc Dimittis was especially moving. But the service was torn in two, and its emotion dissipated, by what the programme announced as THE ORATION. Instead of a man with powerful lungs mounting the pulpit and roundly proclaiming Charles's virtues for all to hear, a chair was placed in the aisle between the choir, and to it was helped Dame Edith Sitwell, her bizarre beauty obscured by a fur coat and a huge black mushroom of a hat. Only her fingers, on which clustered emeralds the size of billiard balls, suggested her customary eccentricities. Having with difficulty extracted her spectacles and adjusted them, she began to read softly from a typescript, in which she several times lost her place. To me, scarcely a third of the way down the church, only an occasional word was audible: to the majority behind me, virtually nothing. Douglas Woodruff, who was sitting in front, told me next day that I hadn't missed much. The whole thing was a grotesque error of judgment.

The service finished at 12.40, and by great luck I immediately got a taxi, in which I dexterously managed my quick change. The National Book League had mercifully saved me some sandwiches and a glass of whisky, and I just had time to knock them back before facing the audience of forty or so, mostly feminine and elderly. I introduced the bookseller, who was supposed to talk for thirty minutes, after which a discussion of the same length should follow. To my horror, after speaking jerkily for *six minutes*, the bookseller dried up and sat down. There was nothing for it but for me to resume, and to keep up some sort of noise until the audience joined in or the bookseller recovered. Somehow I did this, and at the end of the hour I had to apply the closure to what by then was a tolerably lively discussion. Phew!

On Friday Comfort came to London for the evening. We had a good dinner and went to *The Potting Shed*,[1] which we both enjoyed. It's a preposterous play, but up to the end of the second act it's dramatically gripping. The third act is a feeble anticlimax.

As you may have seen, *Time and Tide* looks like closing down next month. This will be a great blow, since I have reviewed detective stories for them uninterruptedly for fourteen years, and have become used to both the books and the money.

John Verney has had a charming letter from 'Strix' about his article and J.V. is arranging a dinner in March where we shall all meet. You must meet him some time. Poor Bernard Darwin, like that Norse hero (was it?), is slowly turning into a tree, and will never attend the Lit. Soc. again. I was always surprised that he was really such a commonplace talker. I remember once at a small party he contributed very little, though not apparently bored, and then some weeks later a *Country Life* article, largely based on this party, was full of humorous, shrewd comment which would have greatly added to our fun, had it issued in speech. Is he like Goldsmith, who once allged that, though he never had sixpence in his pocket, he could draw for £1000? Or Kipling?

How right you are about Emerson. Why has he gone *pro. tem.* so completely down the drain—just as Browning has, who, the Leavises now say, had, if you please, 'an inferior mind and spirit,' which is, surely, just silly? I like E's saying that 'the weak point about good resolutions is the fact that, even while we indulge the luxury of framing them, we know in the background of our minds that the task of carrying them into effect will have to be entrusted to the same old incorrigible law-breaker who has so often betrayed us in the past.'

[1] By Graham Greene.

That has more perception, human nature, and humour than many of G.B.S.'s much better known wisecracks.

Your account of Charles Morgan's memorial service is delicious. Why do very clever people behave so stupidly so often? Couldn't a brother or someone have told E. Sitwell that she is inaudible? As old Henson always averred, illegible writing and inaudible talking are both forms of bad manners—and very tiresome ones. Roger spotted you there, and maintains, *more suo*, that half of you was acutely observing who was or was not there, while the other half was fervently and melodiously proclaiming the desire to fly to the bosom of Jesus. Do you remember Horace Walpole's brilliant description of 'the burlesque Duke of Newcastle' at George II's funeral—holding his spy-glass to his eye with one hand and mopping his tears with the other?

Really your quick-change escapades! And then having to fill in the time (which, in passing, I bet you did jolly well). Don't organisers tell speakers roughly how long they are expected to hold the floor? Don't speakers ask beforehand? There are too many asses about.

Time and Tide yes, tragic—and very bad luck on you. Can *any* decent weekly survive—*John o' London's Weekly, Truth, T. and T.* What squalid times we live in. Nature too is quite mad. The sun is shining, a thickish snow is falling with a strong S.W. slant, though the wind is N.E. Sheer Lewis Carroll.

I am glad about old Churchill. These resilient old men are very heartening. On March 21 I dine with C.M. Wells—his birthday party. He is eighty-seven. But Plum Warner—eighty-four I think—is fearfully fragile and almost transparent. Odd that in his prime he particularly enjoyed the fastest bowling; he can't have weighed much more than the ball propelled by Kortright.

I am posting this on Wednesday, as the postal service here is 'looking both ways for Sunday' as George Bonnor used to say the English bowlers would if he could only remember that balls hit along the ground cannot be caught. He never did learn it. Ruskin said he was physically the finest man he had ever seen. He drank like a fish.

I'm glad to say there seems some hope of a reprieve for *Time and Tide*. I am in close touch with the charming young lady who dishes out the review copies. She tells me that Lady Rhondda has told the staff (who are naturally apprehensive and despairing) that the paper will certainly continue beyond the fatal March 22, and maybe indefinitely. We all breathe again. Did you see all the letters in the current issue? The subscribers may be few, but they are certainly loyal.

Last week was a bad one around here. On Tuesday morning Comfort spent four hours vainly trying to drive herself and five children to her school near High Wycombe, some fifteen miles. After skidding, sticking, being dug out, trying another road, she abandoned the struggle, took the children to their various homes, and eventually got back here frozen, wet, dirty and much agitated. (I don't know if I ever told you, but she suffers from blood-pressure so high as to be scarcely credible, which leads to periodical collapses, despite the quieting (and depressing) drugs which she is given by the doctor.) Clearly she was in a bad way when she got home, and the first letter she opened was one from Fred saying that Adam had been flogged by the Headmaster for helping another boy with his Maths Extra Work after twice being warned not to. Comfort has always had a horror of corporal punishment, and of the children being beaten, so this news, coming as it did, was the last straw. Poor darling, she collapsed completely, with nausea, giddiness and general weakness. She rang up Soho Square, but I had gone out to lunch, with a meeting afterwards, so heard nothing till the evening. She was quite alone here, and mercifully she had the sense and strength to drive over to a friend a mile or so away, where she stayed for forty-eight hours. This was just as well, since this house was cut off for the whole of that time—and her school too. I did what I could to reassure her on the telephone, and wrote to Adam telling him to do the same. He rang her up on Thursday, very cheerful, but even that didn't restore her. She got to school on Thursday and Friday, but directly I got down I took her to the doctor, who gave her some magical pills called Purple Hearts. I imagine they are made of Benzedrine or some such stimulant: God knows what they'll do to her blood-pressure, but they have removed all the other symptoms.

To-day we drove over and took Adam out to lunch at Bray. He was well and cheerful, and clearly not bowed down by either guilt or shame. He told us all about his crime. He is in C. Select for Maths (not bad considering he's only fourteen and a half), and in his Tutor's is a lad called X.Y., who is (clearly quite wrongly) in D. Select. He was apparently quite incapable of solving the problems he had to do out of school, and was so worried by his inability that Adam helped him. The warnings were not given to them specifically, but to the Maths divs in general. I pointed out to Adam the folly of this action, since he clearly couldn't carry X.Y. for the rest of his schooldays, and the sooner he's moved down to a div. within his capacity, the better. Adam was entirely frank and philosophical about the whole episode, which has clearly done him no harm. Comfort is, I think, finally re-assured, but I have asked Fred to send any further bad news (pray heaven there is none) to Soho Square. In fact he knows perfectly well I'm there all the week, and didn't think. Sorry to inflict all this on you, but it has naturally filled most of my week. And now I am supposed to write a 'Profile' of Diana Cooper for next week's *Sunday Times* in 350 words—an almost impossible task, which I haven't yet begun. Have I sent you the Wells-James book? Clearly not, but I will. I am reading *Sartor Resartus*, which is as clotted as Colin Wilson but much more rewarding.

6 March 1958   *Grundisburgh*

What a perfectly detestable time your poor lady and you must have had! I positively ached with sympathy as I read it, and so did Pamela. When we came to the execution of Adam, she, with that contempt for men's laws and that clear commonsense which all good women share, said 'Why did they want to flog him for that? Don't they approve of kind acts?' And somehow the case one puts up for the necessity of rules, and hard cases making bad law etc, invariably sounds rather thin and mean. I hope Birley had the sense to make it a token flogging

27

so to speak—and anyway I hope Comfort now sees that she has fundamentally been given additional reason for being proud of her son. Just before I took on Brinton's, a boy, moved to the heart's core by a sermon, went out onto Slads and presented a tramp with his new shirt and of course got six of the best from the captain of the house. Brinton, that worthy old sadist, told me the tale with glee. However God defeated Mammon in the end as the boy became a parson. The last time I saw him, I think the tramp had given him back his shirt, having found a better one on a scarecrow.

Last night I began the James-Wells book. What a little *cad* H.G.W. became when his temper was lost, and how easily he lost it—in the most literal sense, because everything he then said or wrote was untempered, e.g. to label poor old Percy Lubbock as a 'pretentious, academic greaser' who showed 'extravagant dirtiness' in boycotting Rebecca West's article on H.J. is surely right off the map. P.L. was never the *T.L.S.* editor, and what evidence is there that he had anything to do with what articles were or were not inserted? (By the way, might it not be a good thing to extract and print P.L.'s *T.L.S.* reviews? There must have been a good many, and the quality of them was very high. Arnold Bennett once said in one of his *Evening Standard* causeries that there was a man writing in the *T.L.S.* about Henry James in such a way that he had decided never to write another word about H.J. himself. Percy said A.B.'s remark *could* be construed as a condemnation, but, as Field Marshal Robertson said to the Cabinet, 'Well, I think different.')

I am always fascinated by the flexibility and rich resource of H.J.'s vocabulary and phrasing, even if he is saying only 'I hope to call on you some day', but I am surprised at his incomparably acute sensibility not spotting that he puts 'so' before too many adjectives and adverbs. Hypercritical? Perhaps.

I met F.L. Lucas once and liked him very much. I didn't notice his deafness (it was fifteen months ago). Have I a voice like Trollope's which brought the putty rattling out of the windows? *Of course* he ought to have been in the Johnson Club years ago—and David Cecil too. I liked his review of H.J. and H.G.W. in the *Sunday Times*. (By the way what an outstandingly attractive appearance, binding, print etc all your books have. I suspect you have always made a special point of all that. And how speedily your books are dealt with by reviewers. Quite rightly!)

I am delighted to hear you are re-reading *Sartor* which I shall at once do myself. It has superb things in it—the picture of London at night, the Alps ('a hundred and a hundred savage peaks') and the reduction to uttermost simplicity of such things as war ('What quarrel had these two men? Busy as the devil is, not the smallest', but they proceed to blow each other's brains out), and justice—Judge in red, man in the dock in blue. Red says to blue, 'You be hanged' and blue accepts it meekly and *is*. I don't quote—merely recollect from undergraduate days. It is odd to realise that so many professed lovers of literature fail to see, with all its blemishes, the enormous power (*yes*, and *fun!*) of Carlyle's writing. The 'pig philosophy' in *Latter-Day Pamphlets* makes one laugh out loud. And I wish your chap who anthologised him had put in more of his excellent letters (only G.W.L. and Max B. have realised how good *they* are! He said so while eating a *filly de sole* at Butterwick's table in 1943).

9 *March 1958*   *Glyn Felin, Neath, Glamorgan*

Comfort faithfully forwarded your letter, and it reached Soho Square before I left yesterday. The train was so cold that in my first-class carriage (ticket paid for by W.H. Smith, the sponsors of the so-called Brains Trust) I wore my greatcoat and muffler for the whole four and a half hours and shivered withal. I am staying with the octogenarian and stone-deaf (but nevertheless delightful) widow of a tinplate magnate, who lives in this huge and arctic house with her unmarried daughter. In the old days they had five indoor and five outdoor servants: to-day they spend most of their time clearing up after themselves and the one grudging woman who works for them. It is snowing hard, and I have visions of the rest of the Brains Trust being held up, and my having to hold the audience single-handed for upwards of an hour. Not that I anticipate many turning up at half-a-crown a head. Hitherto I have always performed for helpless schoolchildren, dragooned into the hall. The full horror shall be reported to you on Tuesday.

So glad you're enjoying the Wells-James book. I've had an amusing letter from Percy Lubbock about the reference to him: you shall see it on Tuesday. I feel pretty sure P.L. would say his *T.L.S.* reviews were too unpolished for book-publication, though you and I would probably disagree.

Clearly your trumpet-notes crashed through F.L. Lucas's deafness, which has deterred feebler talkers for twenty years.

I am appalled to read in the current number that *Time and Tide* needs £450 *a week* to keep it going! How on earth can they secure that?

I am thoroughly enjoying *Sartor*, but my word, you have to dig out the nuggets! All those capital letters, German words, and the number of lines beginning with inverted commas must deter the faint-hearted. At Balliol in my day all Freshmen had to read a weekly essay to the Master or some other don. My first week the alternative subjects were Proportional Representation and *Sartor Resartus*. The first I didn't (and still don't) fully understand, and the second looked to me unreadable, so with the utmost pusillanimity I went sick.

I fear that note on Diana Cooper was poor; I struggled with it for days: the most difficult bit of writing I've ever attempted. Forgive this scrap. Tuesday 6.

10 March 1958   *Grundisburgh*

Sickening! We are so infested with climatic vagaries that I cannot leave Pamela to cope with them alone—pipes threatening to freeze, snow to seep through, and the moment a thaw comes the certainty of a flooded cellar and possibility of the automatic pump sticking. Like all pumps it is as temperamental as a prima donna. Only yesterday we exhorted ice and snow to praise the Lord, but alas the Lord's all-seeing eye spotted that I thought this exhortation ridiculous, so sent us an extra packet.

I am particularly sorry to miss this meeting, as I should have liked to add my welcome to old Jonah, but there it is.

I telephoned to No 36 this morning and a bright feminine voice said it would be all right *qua* the Garrick and warning them, and your secretarial soul will not be excoriated by having a dinner for seventeen and only sixteen guests to eat it.

And I had *so* much to talk to you about. Damn!

Your Wales trip doesn't sound to have been pleasant, but I always regard you as one of those highly—and justly—praised by the psalmist, who, 'going through the vale of misery, use it for a well'. How deliciously characteristic that you should have been staying with the stone-deaf widow of a tinplate magnate. As to Lucas's deafness, and my not noticing it, I am afraid your diagnosis may be too kindly. I suspect he spotted that my conversation was not such as he need pay much attention to, and it would do to meet it with those inarticulate murmurs which H.G. Wells described as resembling responses in church. Have you read F.L.L.'s book?[1] I haven't yet. There was the sort of review I particularly dislike by John Raymond in the *New Statesman*, but I have a suspicion that L. *does* rely on too many quotations, apt as they always are. What do you think? His width of reading seems to be enormous—in several languages (but I wish he would translate his quotations from Italian and Spanish). And I look forward to making the same protest to P.-J. at the next Lit. Soc. Did you read that grim article on medieval Spanish playwrights some weeks ago?

I was interested to read in *Punch* that Anthony Powell always found H.G.W. unreadable. Odd—but I suppose to *his* generation W's speculations and prophecies and impatient omniscience were all becoming rather tarnished. *My* generation simply battened on him—not so much, in my case at least, his prophecies etc as his humour and frequent penetration. Who was the man at some wedding breakfast who 'had just taken a mouthful that amounted to conversational suicide'? And I bet old H.J. savoured such things too. But, Gosh, how dead H.G.W.'s books are now, while H.J.'s are not—though I gather in the man Amis's last novel, a character surveying another's shelves, and reading the titles, bursts out '*Portrait of a Lady*! Oh my God!' But even the youth of 1958 will soon be finding out that what Amis—with

[1] *The Search For Good Sense* (1958).

many others—says doesn't matter at all. I look forward to hearing what Percy L. said on finding himself labelled 'a greaser'. I believe H.G. *could* be delightful in company, and much must be forgiven to the man who invented the Christian name Altiora for Mrs Bailey, i.e. Beatrice Webb, in *The New Machiavelli*. I cannot help hoping that for a moment it pierced even her armour of self-satisfaction.

How right you are about *Sartor*; it *is* hard going, but as *he* said of Coleridge's monologues, wonderful sunny islets do sometimes emerge from the general haze. I was always attracted by the thrawn old dyspeptic, his poor tummy fermenting with what he (mistakenly) called 'an innocent spoonful of *porridge*' last thing at night. But, gosh, what marvellous pictures he had in his head. Do you remember the account of Robespierre's execution, ending 'Samson, thou canst not be too quick', with the dreadful reason why?

We liked your 'profile' of Diana Cooper, though Pamela—*more feminarum*—observed that her charm in old days was more perceptible to men than to women. Not that she was hinting at anything at all derogatory, but merely that D.C. got the masculine votes more easily than the feminine—which, when I look at it, is rather a bad platitude, bad because it seems to hint at something sinister in the background. But it doesn't—and P. is *never* 'feline', any more than was Hugh Walpole's biographer! (X's book still has not come my way. I am pretty sure I shall dislike *him*, as I always do a writer who is hailed by the 'chorus of indolent reviewers' as 'having no nonsense about him'. One knows at once he is going to throw mud of some sort at better men than himself. And one is *not* prejudiced in favour of a man who describes *Middlemarch* as 'insincere humbug' because the author lived in what one's grandmother called sin with the 'little ape' Lewes. On the whole *M* is my favourite novel. Was it V. Woolf who said it was almost the only grown-up novel of nineteenth-century England?)

I spent a day or two ago among the March monthlies much im- or de-pressed by an article on 'Scriptistics', but immensely cheered by the name of its author, which, believe it or not, is Dr Virgil Wigwam. Probably you know all about 'Scriptistics'? Those who master it (or them?) know *all* the rules about composing poetry. Another article follows it, by a Russian young woman who says—of course—that they have known all about it in Russia for years, and that Dr Wigwam has slipped into several grave errors. Is there *any* limit to the anfractuosities of the human mind?

15th March 1958   *Bromsden Farm*

My Welsh trip was on the whole agreeable, though the Brains Trust itself wasn't much cop. Some three hundred demented citizens had paid half-a-crown each, and they filled rather less than half the hall. The 'panel' consisted of Lionel Hale (in the chair), L.A.G. Strong, Lettice Cooper (a nice Yorkshire novelist), myself, and an ebullient Welsh schoolmaster (and, I gather, television star) called Gwyn Thomas. On him we had to depend for answers of some sort to such questions as: 'Do you consider that the flowering of Welsh literature can be partly explained by the fact that Wales escaped early from the domination of the Roman Catholic Church?' I found it easier to cope with 'Are books too expensive?', while 'What do you consider the greatest novel ever written?' produced a mixed bag of answers. There were preliminary drinks in the Mayor's Parlour, but I managed to avoid the subsequent dinner. Lionel Hale told me next morning that all the Welshmen spoke until the Goddess Reason tottered on her throne, and he had no doubt that any two English doctors would have certified them all *in situ*.

Other Lit. Soccers besides you fell by the wayside on Tuesday, but we sat down eleven. Tommy had Tony Powell and Jimmy Smith beside him, so I took charge of Jonah, who had Leslie Hartley on his other side. Donald Somervell was on my left. Jonah seemed slightly bemused and a trifle deaf, but he ate and drank heartily, and enjoyed talking about quasi-theological literature with Donald. The latter delighted me by telling me that when someone asked Renan whether he was turning Protestant, he replied: 'I have lost my faith, but not my reason'. I expect you knew that already.

I have just read William Plomer's new book *At Home*. Having known and loved W.P. for twenty-six years, I find it hard to judge his books dispassionately, but I enjoyed this one immensely: it was just like listening to him talking at his wisest and wittiest: do try the book. Some of his jokes are first-rate, like his translating 'near-miss' to a Frenchman as *demi-vierge*.

I don't think Tony Powell is wholly representative of his generation in his attitude to Wells. I am only a year or two younger than Tony, and in my youth I lapped up H.G.'s novels. *Mr Britling* was the first wholly adult modern novel I ever read, and I was as impressed with it as with my own advancement. What should I think of it to-day? One day I must try.

I realise that the profile of Diana wasn't nearly good enough, but it filled the space and delighted Lord Kemsley (owner of the *Sunday Times*), who called his staff together and told them it was the best one they'd had for years! Since they had written most of the others, they received his words somewhat sourly. Diana too was pleased, though horrified by the photograph. In a postcard from Rome she wrote: 'Glass[1] should be broken, and whoever wrote the praise exhalted.' (Her spelling is always her own.)

I am writing this on Saturday, because tomorrow morning I have to drive to London Airport to meet my American friend Leon Edel, the great Henry James expert (have I sent you the first volume of his biography of H.J.? He is now at work on the second). I'm bringing him here for the night, and taking him up on Monday to the flat, where he will stay, off and on, till April 5. Perhaps he'd enjoy the Johnson Club? You'd certainly like him.

I shall think of you carousing with C.M.W. on Friday. I am eagerly watching *The Times* for your next grandchild—'and still they come'. Have you any daffodils in flower? We have a few in bud, threatened by frost and ice. Poor Comfort had toothache all last week, on top of all her troubles, but to-day all is well. Duff comes home from Oxford on Thursday; their terms are all too brief; I only hope he will do some work in the garden.

20 March 1958   *Royal Empire Society*

I am at the furthest pole from the summer-house—the large and stuffy lounge of my club, among coal-black bishops talking volubly no doubt about God in various languages, all of which resemble the

[1] Douglas Glass, the photographer.

cries of alarmed cock-pheasants. Two are wearing tight skull-caps which, as no doubt you know, contrive to give the most saintly a criminal aspect. Is there some sect which regards a bald head as indecent exposure? Your Welshmen sound pretty garrulous too. Is there a great efflorescence of Welsh literature? It hasn't reached East Anglia yet. But if the idiom is that of that *delicious* book *How Green was my Valley* I hope it soon will. I don't think I have ever heard your opinion of that masterpiece. I wish R. Llewellyn would write a sequel to it, though I rather respect him for not doing so.

Jonah obviously enjoyed his first Lit. Soc. evening immensely, though a little distressed at the early departure of the older members, recalling the Doctor's dictum that any man who goes to bed before twelve is 'a scoundrel' (I have, not for the first time, the grim suspicion that I have told you all this before, and I can't look up your penultimate letter to see). I must get W. Plomer's book; it sounds good value. Is there *any* man of contemporary letters whom you *don't* know? *Demi-vierge* is brilliant. I am glad you are not an anti-H.G.W. H.J.'s admiration of his enormous richness and vitality was clearly deep and genuine, but I suppose with that up-bringing he could never get rid of all the chips on his shoulder. I should have liked to tell him what a grand bowler my father said his father was nearly a hundred years ago. Or did he regard bowling as G. Meredith regarded tailoring?

I say, London!! A dreadful place to live in. I sit in the Underground, deeply depressed by the scores of clayey faces all round me, 'all silent and all damned'[1] surely—absorbed in evening-papers but showing no sign of enjoyment, interest or any reaction whatever. And my seat is always opposite one of those emetic advertisements of Amplex. Last night at the rush hour I nowhere near got a seat and was almost flattened by the press. No one got out between Tottenham Court Road and Archway, where *all* got out. Does every clerk and typist etc live in Highgate? I had never heard of Archway till it became my brother's station.

Edel's Vol I is about the only book you have not sent me of all your rich output. Why not bring him to the Johnson Club? A good man—especially an American—*ought* to see J's house. I think it might be one of the better evenings with Roberts and Christopher Hollis—who

[1] Wordsworth, 'Peter Bell'.

now for some reason as obscure to him as to me has to sign his *Punch* articles Percy Somerset. Editors are strange folk.

We had a good week-end. Diana has produced a son and is over the moon with joy, and so is her good man. And on Monday Humphrey defeated the Barnet R.D.C. over his 'cowshed'. The surveyor was fool enough to say his proposed house was 'anti-social', which slow full-pitch was duly despatched to the boundary by H's law-man saying that a house deliberately designed to enable him to trumpet away without annoying the neighbours was about as non-anti-social as anything could be. And the hanging-judge cordially agreed.

I agree with you about the ridiculous brevity of university terms. The sums paid for twenty weeks' residence p.a. are extortionate. And I do wish the doings and sayings of Oxford striplings were not always front-page news. The young men can hardly help thinking themselves very important.

I have had two school G.B. meetings this week—not very interesting. The last thing ever discussed is education, and my views on finance and architectural plans are practically non-existent; nor have I ever really fathomed the difference between direct-grant schools and grant-aided, or whether it is or is not better to have a three-stream entry or a two-stream. The educational world is in labour with a scheme to prevent the Labour Government from mucking-up the public-schools, but I expect it will be stillborn. The Archbishop of Canterbury is a very good chairman of the G.B.A. and a charming man, but I suppose fundamentally a light-weight. Do you think he ought to have said to my brother recently (who told him a son of Geoffrey Fisher's had been in my brother's battery) 'And who the devil are you'? Very genially and all that, but can you hear Anselm or Sancroft or Temple saying it? 'Sir, this merriment of parsons is mighty offensive'.

The black bishops are sunk in slumber and are not looking or sounding their best; the waistcoat of one is sprinkled with cigarette-ash. Down below-stairs the Lord Alanbrooke is discoursing to a large audience on birds. I am afraid you may think this short measure, but my ideas flow more freely in the summer-house where there is no bishop, or babble, or snore, or Amplex—nothing but a score of daffodils, a robin or two (and of course an occasional flake of snow).

All last week I was busily occupied with Leon Edel. He is the most intelligent, charming and undemanding of men, but he hasn't been in England for twelve years and was clearly agog for literary and other society, so I did my best.

On Tuesday I dined him at the Garrick and took him on to a party at Rosamond Lehmann's, where he scored a right and left with the American Ambassador, Mr Whitney, and T.S.E., very mellow in his wedded bliss. Also present were Stephen Spender, Dadie Rylands, Hester Chapman, together with sundry wives and extras.

On Wednesday I went as a guest to the dinner of the International P.E.N. at the Criterion Restaurant. I sat between the elderly wives of the Esthonian Minister and the French Chargé d'Affaires. They were both very nice, but conversation was laboured until the Esthonian began in the greatest detail to tell me about her thrombosis. They had just got her into the ambulance when the speeches began. A French writer called André Chamson made a good speech (in French) which included a moving tribute to Charles Morgan and some good jokes. He said that wherever he goes he is asked the same two questions: '*Qu'est ce que vous pensez de Françoise Sagan?*' and '*Qu'est ce que vous pensez des Jeunes Gens Furieux?*' Then Leon Edel made a brief and fitting speech, Richard Church a long flat one, and then a ghastly bearded Scottish Nationalist professor spoke for what seemed hours. The Scotch *are* tiresome people, aren't they? Particularly when they're trying to be funny. 'I'm sorry to disappoint the ladies by not coming in my kilt—not that I've pawned it'—and so on interminably.

Next day I took Leon to a lunchtime lecture at the National Book League, on T.J. Wise by a reputedly redoubtable librarian from Texas called Fannie Ratchford. She proved mild and nervous, and said nothing new. All the bibliographical and bookselling boys were there, so that the discussion afterwards was better than the lecture.

On Friday I gave a Jamesian luncheon-party for Leon in the small private room at the Garrick. There were eight of us, and I think it was a great success. Now Leon is spending the week-end at Ewelme with the Nowell-Smiths, and is to rejoin me on the train tomorrow morning. (It is late and I am writing this so fast that I fear the sentences don't construe: pray forgive.)

I have never read *How Green was My Valley*, but almost thou persuadest me.

Lord Kemsley, still delighted with my snapshot of Diana C., rang up to ask me to do to-day's on Celia Johnson. I begged off, and suggested Bernard Fergusson, who wrote most of it, though the insertion of theatrical details of which he was ignorant rather spoiled its shape.

27 March 1958   *Grundisburgh*

No, it won't do![1] It is all very well for our stout eupeptic secretary to say that a fork supper (at £1.0.0 per head!) does not cause him a moment's embarrassment, but it ought to. And that hugger-mugger collecting of chairs at literally the last moment—was dear Dr Powell supposed to sit on the floor? It wasn't otherwise a *very* good evening. The paper was all right (was it *conspicuously* above B+?); and I wanted to have *you* within conversational range, though both Roberts and Hollis were excellent value (Roberts's little speech I thought the best thing of the evening). Were the many parts of that American's speech that I couldn't hear a) better, or b) worse than the parts I did hear?—which I wished the Doctor himself could have heard, and we should have had something to put beside his advice to the young man to have his head fumigated, 'for that is the peccant part'. And I should have done better with you and Roberts afterwards. Hollis was all right, Sir Russell was amiable but rather watchful and silent, and that nice, richly-stomached guest of Hollis's, whose name I have forgotten, was fighting a losing battle against sleep most of the time. Hollis is a good Johnsonian, by which I mean his annoyance about the catering sprang from a sense of insult, not to his stomach, but to the Doctor and the Club. Nobody will bring a guest to such meagre entertainment, but I fancy I saw that crusading glint in your eye, which the committee of the London Library knows and trembles before—in fact you have already got to work and roped in two new

[1] The recent dinner of the Johnson Club.

38

members who are sound in wind and limb and under seventy. Good Dr Chapman would have pursed his lips over them, I feel.

John Verney gave us an excellent dinner, and it really was a good evening, not ending till 12—except for Peter Fleming who came in 'faultless evening dress' (with medal-ribbons) as he had to go to some posh reception. He and J. Verney seemed to get on very well. I sat next to Lord Altrincham, who seemed an extremely pleasant fellow—much younger than I expected; John Murray the publisher, whom no doubt you know, and John Bayley of New College, an old pupil of mine, who writes poetry and criticism well above the head of his erstwhile tutor, and is married to Iris Murdoch, who, according to him, has far superior brains to his own. You would like him—in fact you would have enjoyed the evening and I wish you had been there.

I look forward very much to hearing what you think of *How Green*. I *cannot* believe you won't enjoy the English—or how you can fail to fall in love with Bron. When is your birthday and where?—your Yorkshire fastness, I suppose. I have no meetings for a month (except the Lit Soc—unless these blasted strikers dish that) and then we are soon in June when the dreariest of all ceremonies—school prize-givings —are thick on the ground. Tell me what to say to the boys of Bromsgrove, which will divert them from a career of crime and the weekly perusal of *Reveille*, which I heard an elderly man once sum up as 'all bosh and bosoms' which, however, doesn't distinguish it from many other journals.

I expect you have noted the death of my beloved half-aunt Mrs Alington. She was much crippled, and generally speaking full of broken machinery, but she had got home, after a week or two's nursing-home, went to bed and placidly failed to wake up. She was as good a human being as one could hope to meet.

Isn't there something in *Sartor* about how we 'haste stormfully across the astonished earth'? Never for a moment did Carlyle forget the mystery and the brevity and the incongruity of human life. A trait which I always liked in him. In fact all writers ought to have it—not necessarily *ever* to appear.

The Henry James biography Vol I arrived just before I left. In a minute I am going in to tea, then I shall open that delicious parcel—

and gloat. (Is there any greater pleasure?) I shall start reading it the moment I have finished *Middlemarch*, of which there are still 250 pages (out of 1200—one of the very few books that really are long enough). According to old Saintsbury very few are; he must be the only man who ever lived who wanted more of *The Faery Queen*. Have you read any of it? I once managed about ten pages and have ever since rested content with that.

I agree with all your strictures on the Johnson Club. I've no doubt that I *could* get it right, but I simply haven't the time. Why shouldn't the Club own its own liquor? Even that pitiable and extravagantly dear collation the other night could have been taken at the accustomed long table. Certainly no-one would twice inflict such pigging on a guest, and I can see some looming resignations as well. When Williams (the President) gets back, I'll have a go at him.

I'm planning to take three weeks' holiday immediately after the Fourth of June, in my Yorkshire fastness (don't tell Roger). There, apart from reading *Middlemarch* and *How green etc*, I hope to polish off the introduction to the Wilde letters, so that I can send the whole caboodle to the printer in July. But no doubt my reach exceeds my grasp—or is it the other way round?

I was so sorry to read of the death of Mrs Alington. I never knew her, but she was in every sense a great figure in my youth, and I never heard any but good words of her. You have unerringly put your finger on Carlyle's greatest quality—that constant feeling of man in relation to the mysterious immensities of the Universe—and one can forgive him a lot of his crotchetiness on that account.

Stephen Potter once wrote of George Saintsbury: 'It is recorded that for eighteen years he *started the day* by reading a French novel (in preparation for his history of them)—an act so unnatural to man as almost in itself to amount to genius.' He also quotes G.S. as writing in his *History of Criticism*: 'Grillparzer's natural limitations appear to have been further tightened by his playwrightship and by the influence of Joseph Schreyvogel, a sort of Austrian Nisard, of whom I do not know so much.' Both these splendid passages are to be found in S.P.'s entertaining book *The Muse in Chains*, a history of the teaching of Eng. Lit., published by Cape in 1937, when I was there. In it you will find, among many diverting details, the fact that F.D. Maurice was responsible for introducing Chaucer's *Prologue* into the syllabus.

On Thursday evening I took Leon Edel to see *Lysistrata* (which they pronounce LISS-ISS-*TRARTER*). It is tolerably amusing with some good bawdy jokes, but would be improved by the removal of much song and dance, which were clearly introduced to pad out the play to something like an evening's worth. I am enjoying Edel's visit very much, and shall miss him when he leaves next Saturday, though I must confess it will be convenient to have a little time for my own work. He is the easiest and most congenial of guests.

The Society of Authors, hitherto poverty-stricken, has come into something like a fortune by getting a small percentage of the royalties of *My Fair Lady*, and is now setting out on a programme of goodwill dinners, designed to bring authors and publishers together informally to discuss matters of mutual interest. The first of these occurred last Wednesday: it began with a dozen oysters each, and continued with bortsch (into which cream and brandy were liberally flung), excellent chicken, sweet and savoury. Two good wines, brandy and cigars. I was between a nice literary agent and Arthur Bryant, who was most agreeable. The idea that monopolised most of the talk was that publishers should pay a voluntary royalty of 1% on all out-of-copy-right books, the money to be put into a fund to help literature, poor or old authors, scholarship etc. Like all such ideas, it is admirable *in theory*. Anyhow Arthur Bryant and I have been detailed to ask Tommy Lascelles—off the record—whether he thinks the Pilgrim Trust could possibly act as trustees to such a fund. Meanwhile I gather that our old campaign for new legislation on Obscenity in Literature (the Herbert Committee) may soon be brought to a victorious conclusion by the Government's bringing in a Bill very like the one we caused to be introduced.

For people to vote Liberal in disgust at the other two parties may be natural, but seems to me pretty pointless. I see no solution, and shall go on voting Tory until something better turns up. *Et toi?*

Your holiday is still a long way off—how you love overwork! I wonder what you will make of *Middlemarch*. Somebody at that Barmecide feast said he used to love it, but, on trying it again recently, could not make any headway in it. And now comes H.G. Wells's byeblow telling us that George Eliot was an impostor; he is reviewing her letters, in which he sees 'the slow perfection of a technique of self-deception that in the end equipped its possessor to become a perfect supplier of soft solder to *l'homme moyen sensuel*, the swamped and ignoble Tartufe (sic) of industrial society'. To which, as was once said, the only answer is 'resonant, monosyllabic, and plural'. For her great admirers were people like Mr Gladstone, Tennyson, Leslie Stephen, Birrell etc. It is true that old George Moore called her intellectuality 'studied brag', but that might have been expected. But what made Ruskin write 'that disgusting *Mill on the Floss*'? He may have been just about to go off his head—or have just gone. Of course one may well be derisive of all that solemnity, as of some sibyl receiving a string of worshippers, but I doubt if among them were to be found many *hommes moyen sensuels*. A. West like so many clever young men (but *is* he so young?) is much better—often good in fact—about what or whom he admires than on those *unsympathisch* to him, when, *me judice*, he often drivels. All he writes is from the personal angle—about the authors, not about their books. He gives you a pretty good chit apropos of Hugh Walpole, whose weaknesses of course he sees, but not much more. Your life 'told with tact and a feline discretion,' he says, is 'much more interesting than anything H.W. managed to write'—which I agree with, but I have never been a great novel-fan. He shows no signs at all that he thinks Maugham's 'Alroy Kear', depicted just at the moment when it would do H.W. most harm, the action of a cad. Surely the really final thing to be said about H.W. by people like God, R.H-D., G.W.L. etc is that he was a much nicer man than most of his detractors, and did a great many very kind actions. I do wish more critics had the art of indicating defects in others without contempt, or complacency ('I haven't such failings'). But perhaps that wouldn't please their public.

The other book I got from the library yesterday was Lord Elton's biographical sketch of Bishop King of Lincoln—certainly the most saintlike man I ever saw: it was unmistakable. Nothing solemn about him, or hearty either. I once stayed with my aunt's husband, Bishop Talbot, at Kennington, and the rest were Bishop Gore, Bishop Paget, Bishop Lang, Scott Holland, Tommy Strong of Christ Church and Bishop King. I was twenty-two; it was great fun. They all had the greatest admiration and affection for old King, but, led by Gore, drew a delicious and convincing picture of him (in his presence) as a worldly, grasping materialist, of low tastes and habits, sipping beer of an evening and falling asleep in his chair, after giving out that he always had an hour's meditation before retiring. Old King played up splendidly, and admitted that there often seemed to him no better place to end his days in than 'a small public-house on the Harrow Road'. You would have loved it, but Anthony West would probably have been quite certain they were all hypocrites, and King an *homme moyen sensuel*. A young cleric, elected to serve on some committee, arrived late and frightened at its first meeting. Old King in the chair, an atmosphere of the heaviest solemnity, only one seat left, next to him. The youth stood appalled, but K. beckoned him to the chair next his, and as he sat down bent and whispered to him behind his hand 'We aint so good as we look'. But probably these mild tales of clerical life bore you? It is very probable that you have never really come across a saint. Blunden has something of the look of one, I thought more than once. Is that right off the target? Oh, but yes, you have, i.e. Mrs Alington; she certainly wasn't far off. That thing of Robert Birley's in *The Times* was first-rate. The only thing lacking to a complete picture was her magnificent *wrath* at anything mean or vulgar. I remember a film in the School Hall in which the whole and sole point was that nearly everyone in it was drunk. She came out at the end, her face crimson and lowering, and standing on the steps in her bell-of-doom voice cried 'Damn,' and added a few blistering words about the results of long and expensive education. She had latterly every kind of ache and pain, and lameness and blindness, and never paid the smallest attention to any of them. She was the last of that generation, her eldest half-brother being my father, born in 1842.

I like that saying about old Saintsbury, a man no one surely could help liking and respecting; that tremendous gusto for everything in life and literature from sandwiches to Swinburne. I remember hearing Housman say (after some pretty sharp words about S's style) that it was meritorious—a *very* high word of praise on A.E.H.'s lips—that anyone who wrote so much was so rarely off the mark in his literary judgments. Do you agree with his dictum that whenever you are offered fried sole, whatever may be the alternatives, fried sole should be your choice? I do rather, but C.M. Wells, though not antagonistic to this view, said that in his opinion cold ham was the only thing that deserved such a high place in the list. But he admitted that there must be nothing wrong with the feeding, the killing, the curing, the cooking, and the carving. I do like food, don't you, though, unlike Agatha Christie, we shall never say so in print? What is that love-poem which ends

> Seared is of course my heart, but unsubdued
> Is and shall be my appetite for food?

It was one of Mrs A's few weaknesses that food to her was mere fuel. I remember her vivid ejaculations, three quarters horror one quarter reluctant laughter, at an advertisement of some restaurant, one man glossy and taut with food and wine saying to another: 'Well, I think that's the best dinner I've ever eaten.'

That is lovely—'Joseph Shreyvogel, of whom I do not know so much'. G.S. must have been about the last of the polymaths. Do any of the Youngs and Bryants and Toynbees qualify? Who are these illiterate producers who always get names wrong? Lysistrata for instance, and I remember in the *Caesar and Cleopatra* film Britannus was always Brittanus, just as *every* lower boy for some reason used to pronounce Achilles as a dactyl. We have a good man on the County Council here who never will let pass controversy (as in 'of') or hospitable. The only really sensible change in my lifetime has been 'laboratory', which, when I was young, was practically indistinguishable from lavatory, and now isn't. Except for the trivial circumstance that now no children are starving or ragged, practically all other changes have been for the worse!

I believe I have been more intolerably lengthy than ever. This paper? I know you like a juicy sentence. Here is what Meredith said in a letter of old Carlyle: 'Swim on his pages, take his poetry and fine grisly laughter, his manliness, together with some splendid

teaching . . . I don't agree with Carlyle a bit, but I do enjoy him.'
And 'He speaks from the deep springs of life . . . but when he would
apply his eminent spiritual wisdom to the course of legislation, he is
no more sagacious nor useful nor temperate than a flash of lightning
in a grocer's shop.' Perfectly true—and the grocer's standpoint
steadily ousts the seer's, and Mrs Sidney Webb rests in the Abbey
and Carlyle at Ecclefechan.

Easter Sunday, 6 April 1958   *Bromsden Farm*

In the snowstorm I began to fear that I should never get Leon Edel
to the airport, but all was well. Somehow Comfort managed to pick
him a bunch of daffodils, which, he reports this morning in a cable
from New York, stood the crossing well. I shall never grow accustomed to the annihilation of time and space. Leon's three weeks' stay
has been a great pleasure, but I had to spend most of my spare time in
his service, to the detriment of the long-suffering Oscar.

Adam redeemed his misdeed by once again doing well in Trials: he
just missed a Distinction (scoring 997 instead of 1000) but carried off
the Trials Prize for Lower C—which I call good at 14.8. He spent his
prize-money on a one-volume Shakespeare, *The Faber Book of Comic
Verse* and T.S.E.'s *Old Possum*—quite a good choice, and he said there
wasn't much else in the shop worth having. Apparently Fred
Coleridge is going to move into the new house as soon as it's ready:
the boys are being told that its inaccessibility and lack of a squash
court will be set off by central heating and (some say) hot and cold
water in every room!

I do indeed love food, and certainly put fried sole very high on the
permanent list.

Those bits of Meredith on Carlyle are superb: where do they
occur? I have won through to the end of *Sartor*, and am now em-
barked on *Heroes*. You always know the bits I send you, but here's one
on *Fashionable Novels*:

Of such Sacred Books I, not without expense, procured myself
some samples; and in hope of true insight . . . set to interpret and
study them. But wholly to no purpose: that tough faculty of

45

reading, for which the world will not refuse me credit, was here for the first time foiled and set at naught . . . At the end of some short space, I was uniformly seized with not so much what I can call a drumming in my ears, as a kind of infinite, unsufferable, Jew's-harping and scrannel-piping there; to which the frightfullest species of Magnetic Sleep soon supervened. And if I strove to shake this away, and absolutely would not yield, there came a hitherto unfelt sensation, as of *Delirium Tremens*, and a melting into total deliquium: till at last, by order of the Doctor, dreading ruin to my whole intellectual and bodily faculties, and a general breaking-up of the constitution, I reluctantly but determinedly forbore.

That's what the old hero wrote where we should say 'The book was unreadable'. I once drove through Ecclefechan, but had no time to drop a tear on T.C.'s grave. My God, what a depressing place!

Easter Monday morning

Another cold, grey, snow-laden-looking day. I shall not stir very far abroad. Adam is off to a point-to-point with a thermos of hot soup and a mass of sandwiches. Comfort is driving him to the house of the friends who are taking him, and the only chance of getting this posted is for her to take it. Hail is now sharply rapping the window.

Last week Eric Linklater turned up, unannounced as usual, and bore me off to lunch at the Savile Club. The food there isn't bad, but it seldom serves to absorb the quarts of liquor which are dispensed at the bar beforehand. As I left, Eric was ordering me a double Kümmel, and if he drank that as well as his own, he must surely have spent the afternoon lying down.

Did I tell you about my dentist? I have been to the same man for thirty-five years, and when he died last year I felt quite lost. Now, through the enterprise of my sister (who always went to the same chap), I am transferred to a charming Canadian, who makes tapestries and seems gentle and efficient. I paid my first visit to him last week, and came away much relieved. I have a horror of false teeth, which I have so far avoided. Martin Secker, the publisher, has still got all his own teeth at about your age.

The new Ian Fleming, *Dr No*, is pretty poor: after a brilliant opening chapter, the whole story becomes so improbable that, although his narrative gift makes one read on, unbelief is not for a moment suspended. I am supposed to devote 500 words to it in the moribund *Time and Tide* ('it's dead but it won't lie down') and don't want to hurt anybody's feelings.

9 April 1958   *Grundisburgh*

Never has spring been so long a-coming—or does one say that four years out of five? Bad year for daffodils they say; anyway only about a quarter of ours are out, and there is hardly a sign of that reddish mist about the trees which precedes the green. And R.L.S. was not saying a word too much when he called the N.E. wind 'snell, blae, nirly, and scowthering'—not that I really know what any of the four words means. I must ask Ivor Brown at the Lit. Soc. on Tuesday. Can you bear that I should drink with you beforehand, as usual? (No answer desired or deserved!)

I should have liked to see something of Leon Edel. Does he know Percy Lubbock? Clive Carey and I tried once at Lerici to find out from him why (if he knew) some not unintelligent people find H.J. positively nauseating, e.g. Swinnerton's friend who said that he was like (1) a formal suet-pudding, and (2) a rat (which is *not* very like a f.s.-p.!) and Laski who described him as 'a second-class mind dealing with fundamentally third-class ideas'. But you may well say (a) Laski was a sh-t (b) like H.G.W. a journalist rather than an artist (c) and liked denigrating. All quite true. But we really got nothing out of Percy—and one evening when we both said one of the H.J. stories—read aloud by me—seemed to be a lot of fumbling and fuss about practically nothing, we saw a not very distant danger-signal and changed the subject. Laski said H.J.'s letters made him vomit, with their excessive affectionateness and gush. Well, there it is our old friend allergy—such for instance as made W. Raleigh hateful to Swinnerton, though most people found him immensely likeable.

Adam sounds to have done well; in any case trials-prize and flogging in the same half I should think is a record. My son-in-law says he is a good boy, and he doesn't praise easily. He (B. Bourne) made himself, he says, very unpopular a fortnight ago at Putney, when he told the Oxford coaches (who were saying that Oxford had improved miraculously into a class crew) that he thought it was a thoroughly poor crew. I watched the race on TV with him. After *one* minute he said 'The race is over'—and it was! It is all very odd. When I was a boy, Cambridge never dreamt of winning the race.

How nice it is to find someone appreciating the flavour of old Carlyle as you do. I always have, but generally find myself in a minority of one. So few recognise *power* when they come across it. They boggle at his 'message' or his politics or religion (just as they do about Kipling's 'imperialism', as if that put *The Jungle Books* and *Captains Courageous* out of court). The Meredith sentence comes from a letter—let me go and find it—yes 1865 (no month or day given) to Captain Maxse.

Ecclefechan is a grim little spot, though I believe much less so than Craigenputtock, which I never saw. I asked a native of E. about Carlyle, and he had never heard of him. And I read some time that soon after his death a native, asked the same question, knew *all* about the others, but as to Tom 'Oh aye there was Tam, but he went up to Lunnon and I never heard as he came to any good'. It was he or another who summed up the whole family as 'pithy, bitter-speakin' bodies', like T's father (not mother) who at family prayers read the story of Joseph and Potiphar's wife, closed the bible and said 'Aye, and thou wast a bitch, woman' in a loud angry voice as if she was sitting there. That passage of T.C.'s about novels is just what I mean by his being full of flavour; all the many feelings the novels had given him are there, distinct and vivid. It reminds me—how shocked the old man would have been!—of what some woman told George Moore she felt in sexual intercourse. Now where on earth did I come across that? You will know. My uncle Alfred was taken to see T.C. in 1878 or 9 by Ruskin, and told us the old man was very dreamy and melancholy and, as R. said afterwards, already half out of this world. My uncle said R. was charming with him, so gentle and motherly. ('Now, now, this is too bad', as someone recorded was often his way of restoring some kind of equanimity. If T.C. despaired of civilisation in 1878, what would he have done in 1958?)

I gather you did not go to the point-to-point, and suspect that you may share my view that it is about the poorest of human pleasures—almost on the level of the sheep-dog trials in Westmorland (though I grant you the pleasure of seeing a dog on one side of a broad valley obeying the inarticulate cries of a shepherd on the other side, about two-thirds of a mile distant).

Your vignette of Eric Linklater calls him up vividly. Is he going to be at the Lit. Soc.? I agree in resenting false teeth, though I have long been in the state of Miss Bobby Bennett's mother 'who imparted to me the surprising confidence that she had only two teeth in her head, but thank God, they met'. It is tragically sad that Œ.E. Somerville lost all her love of the Irish at the end of her life. The rebels had burnt her brother's house, though the S. family had always been popular with the neighbours and done a great deal for them. She was a friend of Mrs Vaughan's and I very nearly met her at Willowbrook. I should have liked to tell her that my father, my sister and I *all* had *The Irish R.M.* at our bedside.

I shall not read Ian Fleming's latest. He has really gone off the rails in the matter of murders and beatings, and tortures, and impossibility, and lust; Bond I thought was becoming a bore in the last book, and must have made it now. Did you read the analysis of *Dr No* in last week's *New Statesman* by Paul Johnson? I was prepared to mock at P.J. but couldn't help thinking that, if his résumé was accurate, the boot was on the other leg.

13 April 1958   Bromsden Farm

Whoreson is too gentle a word for this penetrating and incessant wind. I daresay your summer-house trapped the sun to-day, but here the blast mocked the sunshine, though the boys manfully got the motor-mower into action. By hugging the library fire I have managed to drag Oscar another fifty footnotes towards completion. My present knowledge of the Parisian underworld of letters in the late Nineties would fill an issue of the *News of the World*, though all dates and facts are hard to pin down. I have also read (or at any rate plodded glumly through) Stephen Potter's new and allegedly funny manuscript. *Gamesmanship* made me laugh a lot, and its two successors were just good enough (all three still sell prodigiously), but the world has moved (deathwards, you may say) in the last ten years, and Potter hasn't budged an inch. In truth the joke is played out, but he won't face the fact. This manuscript consists of a bunch of marginal articles, written during the past six years and slung together with the minimum of care. What am I to say to him? Some dreary compromise, I suppose—what a bore!

On point-to-points (or points-to-point), my dear George, we think as one. I'm thankful to say I've avoided all such for twenty-five years, but my children's appetite for them seems insatiable. On the other hand I have *never* been to a sheepdog trial, and would much like to, just once, preferably on my beloved Yorkshire moors. The ordinary farmers there can make their dogs do anything by long-range whistles, and I'd love to see them in competition with others. After that I daresay it might pall.

I never met Miss Somerville either, but I corresponded with her, and won her approval by playing up to her belief that Miss Ross was still collaborating with her *d'outre tombe*. I fancy Miss S. was a great spiritualist in her latter days.

Last week, walking to the London Library, I passed the little dead-end called Apple Tree Yard, between Jermyn Street and St James's Square. William Nicholson had a fine studio there for many years, and I was often a visitor. His great delight was to give one lunch in a tiny dark harness-room (the whole place had been a stable)—either herrings or lobsters, both of which were obtained from an adjacent fishmonger's with the splendidly eighteenth-century name of Dash & Bellamy. The shop is still there, but its name has marched downhill with the Common Man.

Don't you love names of pith and character? Our Henley butcher (though long run by others) retains its original name, Gabriel Machin, and the pleasure of writing it helps to alleviate the boredom and irritation of the monthly cheques.

Apropos of names, I here shamelessly copy out a suggestion I made in 1948, in a review of Henry James's *Notebooks*. I had always been struck by the extraordinary names he gave his characters—did ever a novel have such an off-putting start as 'She waited, Kate Croy'?—and ventured this:

50

And then there is the absorbing question of the names. At intervals throughout the notebooks James jotted down lists of proper names, taken it seems mostly from the front page of *The Times*, on which he afterwards drew for his characters. One list, for instance, begins: 'Chattle—Voyt—Podd—Tant—Murrum—Glibbery,' and continues in that style for five lines. What emerges is that when James came to select from these lists he tended more and more to choose a particular kind of name—gritty, aseptic, impersonal—Stant, Verver, Theale, Croy, Strether, Densher, Stransom. Was he determined to avoid the overtones which hung about his contemporaries; in Hardy the romantic-pastoral (Yeobright, Oak, Winterborne, Everdene); in Meredith the flamboyant-aristocratic (Patterne, Feverel, Wentworth, Beauchamp)? Was he deliberately seeking names which might be as near algebraic symbols as possible and yet remain names? Certainly few heroines have been saddled with such rebarbative syllables as Fleda Vetch.

Leon Edel told me afterwards that there was nothing in this theory: James just thought them good and suitable names!

17 April 1958   *Grundisburgh*

As always, a red-letter evening, particularly the hour beforehand (after I have recovered my breath!) which always passes much too quickly. It was the first time I have had Ivor Brown as a neighbour, and found him excellent value—a dry wine perhaps, but full of flavour —and even, as old Carlyle might have put it, of 'unutterabilities'. Did I gather that he has to be careful about his health? He repudiated beer to top the evening with, offered by Bernard F., and said he was going to drink milk at home.

Roger rang me up the next morning and was in good chuckling form after sitting next to old Cuthbert, who was in characteristic mood. He looked morosely towards our end of the table, and said that now he didn't know half the members (i.e. Tim, I.B., you, Bernard F. who have been in the Society for years, and me whom he has known since about 1912). He then mentioned Jonah: 'Of course you realise he'll come every month', which is very shrewd, but surely is not to be regarded as a black mark? However he beamed at me like December sunshine, which I attribute entirely to your having told him what I had said of him (*did* I say it?).

Yes of course you must go to one sheep-dog trial, but if you are with s-d *fans* remember to have a pressing engagement in, at longest, an hour. Then you will enjoy it. It is the third hour which gets one down. Best of all of course is to come accidentally across a fell-side shepherd on, say Helvellyn, giving orders to his dog on Skiddaw. I forget if you are a lover of dogs. Have I ever seen one at Bromsden Farm? I am not really, though I like our sheepdog collie which has a curiously attractive blend of cleverness and absurdity and friendliness—except of course to the postman—and when Pamela is there, pays no attention to anyone else.

Following on—or in the modern jargon further to—our talk about names, the *Daily Telegraph* has a good paragraph this morning which I shouldn't like you to miss, so send it. The Alingtons some years ago found a man at their gate knocked out by a motor-car. Lavinia their doctor-daughter had him brought in and put on a sofa, and then came and told her parents 'Believe it or not, but his name is Gotobed'. Yet I have a feeling that it is not as rare as one might think—like Lord Emsworth's pig-man 'Wellbeloved'. John Christie's game-keeper had the Christian name of Eli, which was quite right in a household where oddity was normal. I am pleased that a leading scientist who once stridently declared 'the spark-gap to-day is mightier than the pen' should be called Hogben. That vast tome of his called *Science for the Million* contains obiter dicta such as 'Time will come when Johnson will be remembered, *if at all, for his ineptitudes*'! I am sure he is a man to whom one can safely apply the adjective 'rebarbative', a word I have never used before and doubt if I ever shall again, any more than I have and shall the word 'ambivalent' which is compulsory in almost any *New Statesman* review.

Old Henry James's ear or touch failed oddly sometimes, as David Garnett pointed out in the introduction to *Fourteen Stories* (perhaps the first book you gave me) when he changed 'He looked like a young soldier on a battlefield' to 'He was all the young soldier on the gained field,' and Rebecca West bluntly says his corrections were often ruinous. Had he a vein of Daddy Wordsworth in him? My son-in-law Bourne has just read your *Hugh Walpole* with great pleasure and many chuckles. He ended by liking H.W., greatly disliking Maugham, and very impatient with H.J.'s tortuous letters. I cannot find in your book any evidence that supports Swinnerton's saying that H.W. 'no longer cared for H.J.' Didn't he merely outgrow the period of tutelage? But I may be quite wrong.

I have been reading a Simenon novel in bed—not a detective story, and, as so often with the modern novel, am put off by the ridiculously acute and comprehensive understanding which most of the characters are said to have of all the complicated feelings behind every word, look, and movement of everyone they are talking to. But all you pundits, I gather, put Simenon very high. If you are a S. fan, tell me what to read of his.

20 *April 1958*   *Bromsden Farm*

That *was* a good evening, wasn't it? It's always a good sign when the club servants think it's time the party ended. I didn't gather what was the matter with I. Brown: he ate quite heartily, but stuck to white wine and refused the savoury. While you were talking animatedly to Jonah and Bernard, I felt it my duty to have a crack with Cuthbert. He was affable, and as usual thawed after a judicious application of melted butter, but I can't say I find him an enlivening companion. He told me that no candidates ever got elected to the Lit. Soc. unless proposed by the President or Secretary, and that for him (Sir C.) to propose anybody was a certain way to ensure his non-election. I pooh-poohed it all, but in fact the second part of his statement is true. Why can it be?

I am definitely *not* a dog-lover, which is why you have never seen one here, but I don't object to other people's, especially in small doses and preferably out of doors. How shocked Pamela will be!

I'm delighted to know of your son-in-law's reading and approving of my book: one expects people (perhaps) to read a book when it's new, but a message like yours six years after publication is most heartening. It's quite false to say that Hugh ceased to care for Henry

James. In the last few years he may not have been quite so assiduous in his attentions, but the War was partly to blame. After H.J.'s death early in 1916 Hugh blamed himself for not having taken more trouble to see H.J. during his last leave from Russia, though in fact the old boy was probably too ill to see anyone.

Yes, I am a Simenon-fan all right, but naturally he has his ups and downs. How could he fail to, writing at least six books a year? Unfortunately I can't now remember which are the best ones, so can't advise you.

Yesterday we all drove to the Cotswolds to lunch with Comfort's stepmother, and on the way I snatched half-an-hour in Blackwell's, where I picked up one or two trifles. Nowadays I find motoring increasingly tiresome—so many cars on the road oblige one constantly to brake, stop and change gear. The first gleams of sun bring out L-drivers like flies out of winter-quarters.

What else can I tell you? On Thursday I lunched with Cecil Beaton at his house in Pelham Place: superlative food served by butler and parlourmaid, and a delightful party of eight, including Margot Fonteyn—a bright, intelligent, gay little monkey. Nowadays I so seldom attend such a luncheon-party in a private house that an occasion like this, besides being highly enjoyable in itself, brings back nostalgic memories of *la douceur de vivre* and the golden age.

On Wednesday I lunched in Soho with Tommy Lascelles and Arthur Bryant, to discuss a new scheme for raising a fund to help authors in difficulties. Also I attended a meeting of learned Counsel in the Temple to discuss Diana Cooper's tax problems, with which I will not bore you. Tax-experts are a new—and not altogether welcome—class of men, though they certainly have their uses.

My daughter is due to arrive on Tuesday on the *Queen Elizabeth*, and everything is swept and garnished for her approach. I must try to see that her young man has adequate access to her when she gets here.

I heard today that my only uncle—my father's elder brother—died yesterday. He had been dotty for years, apparently quite happy in some sort of home unless any of his family visited him, when he went off the deep end. He spent all (or most of) his life in the Colonial Service—Gold Coast, Fiji, and Cyprus. When the mob rose in Cyprus they came first to his house to destroy it. He came out and addressed them, saying: 'I am your friend. I have spent years working for you. If you must burn something, please go and do it somewhere else.' Inspired by his oratory, the mob went straight off and burnt Government House to the ground, whereby Ronald Storrs lost all his books, pictures, carpets and other treasures. I once said to R.S.: 'I'm afraid my uncle was responsible for your losing everything.' Generously he replied: 'We must believe he thought he was acting for the best'. Now it doesn't much matter to either of them.

23 April 1958   *Grundisburgh*

The reign of chaos is not yet at an end in this corner of the world— or in any other, judging by the newspapers. *Is* this the workaday world, or is it some species of fairyland? You will wonder at the question till I tell you a series of facts. Last *Thursday* Pamela was rung up by the B.B.C. and told Humphrey was to be the victim in the 'This is your Life' programme on *Monday*. Would she or I come and take part? No. Could his old nurse or governess? Both dead. His old tutor? Abroad, address not known. His friends? Well, yes, we told them the names we could think of. His sisters? One possibly from Eton, but alas the one who knew him best, Mary, was in Malaya, so of course couldn't come. Oh couldn't she! We'll fly her over, and back. And so they did for her seven or eight minutes with H. We saw the half-hour; it was quite amusing. The best thing in it was H's face when he heard Mary's voice outside. M. says the flight must cost them about £350, and others were flown in from all over England. Does it make sense to you? Didn't Macaulay take a year to get to India? The number of people who watch TV is staggering. I went in to Ipswich yesterday, and *everyone* I met, except two, had seen the show, and reproached me for not being in it. It is obvious that it will soon be regarded as a *duty* to appear if asked. Also that in ten years or less a house without a TV will be as out of date as one without a water-closet.

I am glad at what you say about Hugh W. and H. James. It is quite natural that they met and communicated less often latterly. I am two thirds through the Edel volume. Am I stupid or what in thinking we should have liked H.J. more as an old than as a young man? How odd is the effect of his brother's presence—the merely physical effect —almost as inexplicable as the old King's don found the fact that whenever he played the piano his fire smoked—the cause, not discovered for some time, being that the undergraduate in the rooms above on these melodious occasions climbed out of a window and put a slate over the chimney-pot.

Apropos of what you said of H.J.'s bad names, it is amusing to read (on p 213) that he was highly sensitive about names, and actually said to call someone Kate instead of Katherine might be *fatal* to the story! But why did he think Kate Croy better than Katherine Croy?

Let me know the name of a good Simenon when you remember. After H.J. I embark on Gordon Ray's Thackeray volumes, once again trying to find out why I dislike T. as a man. Is it (in the words of that very far from stupid man Hugh Kingsmill) because of his 'claret and Ecclesiastes melancholy, and nervous insistence on his gentleman-liness'? Something of the kind, I think. I used to love *Esmond*, but I remember P. Lubbock once saying that after a time you 'began to see how it was done' and that spoilt it. He who must not be named[1] has, I believe, the lowest opinion of it.

Motoring. How right you are. It is clear that in fine holiday weather the situation really does approach the impossible. And what of ten years hence? Man will very soon choke himself with his own inventions, quite apart from the explosive ones. Meanwhile the pleasant old crafts like the blacksmith's and the thatcher's steadily diminish. A tree, a yard in diameter, is felled in a few minutes by the motor-chainsaw; it used to take two to four men half the day. The Hagley blacksmith, like Handel's village b., had muscles as strong as iron bands; the head woodman could use an axe with the grace and precision with which Sergeant Troy used his sword.[2] Both would be out of work now, or minding a machine, and whereas old Wolryche (the smith) played draughts of an evening in the Nineties, he would in the 1950s be watching 'Life with the Lyons'.

---

[1] F.R. Leavis.
[2] In Hardy's *Far from the Madding Crowd*.

I'm late starting my letter tonight, because I've just spent a whole hour listening to a broadcast of an interview with Harry Truman. I've always had an immense admiration for him, which this talk only enhanced. I wonder whether you heard it? He seems to me a wonderful argument for the American political system at its best. A little haberdasher from Missouri who had to decide to drop the first atom bomb, to intervene in Korea, to run the Berlin air-lift, to fire General MacArthur—a man of immense courage, honesty and common sense. I only wish he was still there!

Bob Boothby, whom I dined with the other night, told me he'd just seen Monty, newly returned from the U.S.A., who said that Eisenhower is firing on one cylinder and can't string two consecutive sentences together: it really is appalling. Boothby also said that Winston was so decrepit when he went to the House last week that they can't believe he'll last very long. This dinner was at White's, where my usually somewhat glum dinner with my old father was turned into a feast of fun by Bob's presence. He is the best company in the world, though among my father's friends I should say your cousin Oliver ran him close.

Needless to say, the Headmaster has refused Adam permission to come to my father's eightieth birthday lunch. If only Fred had been half as enlightened as G.W.L. he would have given permission himself: it's infuriating.

Your account of Humphrey's television performance is fantastic: if they can really afford to spend such sums fetching supporting members of a half-hour broadcast, what must the stars receive!

When you say Handel's village blacksmith, you must mean *Longfellow's*. Handel's was more harmonious than muscular.

I was very fond of Ronald Storrs. His public manner may have been a trifle pompous, but he had a fine sense of humour and an enormous love of life and letters. Apropos of my book, I asked him whether the sovereign says 'Rise, Sir Ronald' or 'Arise, Sir Ronald.' He answered: 'Although I received my knighthood by cable rather than by accolade, I understand that "Arise" is reserved for the Resurrection.'[1]

[1] In fact the monarch says nothing.

I am still reading Carlyle on Heroes, and some of Max's essays, and some Emerson, and a mass of miscellaneous stuff to do with the 1890s. I got photostats of twelve new Wilde letters from America last week.

30 April 1958 *Grundisburgh*

I agree with you (as so nearly, and I hope not boringly, always) about Truman, who met great seas of derision, pity, patronage, advice, and detailed denigration with unvarying calm, and, without any roaring or lashing of tail, was clearly as brave as a lion, and perfectly clear too about what he meant to do. But I am merely dotting your eyes! (i's). As for poor Ike—one longs for another heart-attack. And one's misgivings about the government of the world are not diminished by this morning's picture of Khruscheff and Nasser smiling at each other across a table. Burke smiling at Hare, Browne at Kennedy,[1] Himmler at Goering.

I sent a copy of *A La Carte*[2] to Ivor Brown, who was fully worthy, and is a man whose praise is worth having (I have of course handed on what he wrote in reply, to Jonah). I.B. said in his letter, after saying, as Jonah did, how much he enjoyed a good long session, 'I had known some dull occasions when people drifted off at 9.30. Rupert and Lascelles have made a great and admirable change' (so there!). Pay *great* attention here. I shall be at my daughter Diana's from 13 to 15 May and she wants you to come and dine on the 14th. They both want to know you, and she thinks that my being there would break any ice you might (though I assured her wouldn't) feel about it. Do take this *very* seriously. They would of course love to have your lady too, but I remember you said week-days in London were no use for her.

Yes Longfellow, of course; Handel's blacksmith never broke into song. I forgot, for a moment, the unwinking editorial eye.

I wish I had met R. Storrs again after Cambridge: he was so obviously worth knowing (he made a crisp appearance in Harold

[1] They were hanged for killing a policeman in Essex in 1927.
[2] By L. E. Jones (Jonah).

Nicolson's *Some People*), and I always noticed that good men (e.g. Alec Cadogan—and indeed James Agate who may not have been good but certainly had an eye for what was) always liked him. He had no business to die so young. All the sayings attributed to him are invariably full of flavour—sensible or witty or both. I had never heard that one about 'arise'. Fancy being able to quote yards of Meredith—of all difficult stuff to memorise; of course, though, both he and your mother went through all 'Love in the Valley' stanza v. stanza like parson and congregation, which Middleton Murry said was cheap, but unfortunately backed his judgment by quoting 'Lovely are the curves of the white owl sleeping', to which someone modestly pointed out that Mr Murry had the right to think so if he chose but there was no reason to suppose Meredith did, since he wrote 'sweeping', a very different kettle of fish (as my father invariably said). That hatred of beauty in verse and indeed in words all through the late Twenties and Thirties is very odd. I remember a letter of George Orwell's in which he maintained that 'loveliness' was a 'mushy' word. I suppose his ear found more satisfaction in the *Brekekekex, co-ax, co-ax* of Aristophanes's frogs.

Next Monday I go to Bromsgrove School to talk to the boys about reading. On Wednesday I shall be at Eton (c/o R.M.A. Bourne Esq, The Briary, E.C.) where I hope to find a letter—in which I want you to say if *you* are a Thackeray fan. Somehow I don't expect you are. I continue to dislike him, but rather less. I mean the man. His early stuff remains intolerably unfunny and foully mushy in places. All that resolute jocularity is very trying, don't you find? Yet the old chap had guts and never threw up the sponge. But too often he makes me hot all over, and I hate heat. (Gosh, what a day—exactly the right temperature, a world of daffodils and bird-song all round me, all the green of exactly the right tint, etc etc—mix according to taste with suitable quotation from almost any major or minor poet. I need hardly say I am in the houseen on which you poured such derision.)

I have just been reading T.S.E.'s latest essays.[1] Very good especially on Milton, Johnson and Kipling—and I expect you will say on Yeats, whose later work always finds me a little out of my depth. T.S.E.'s

[1] *On Poetry and Poets* (1957).

tone is admirable—never scornful or prejudiced, or shallow, or pretentious. A good man.

I must go to supper. There will be haddock cooked in—I think—cream, as Pamela knows how to do it, and a French cheese by no means to be cursorily dismissed. To end, I shall eat a ginger-nut (with my coffee) which must come from Huntley & Palmer and no one else. Then I shall read some more Thackeray with some little bouts of senile sleep—and a Wodehouse short story in bed.

P.S. And bed will not be before midnight.

Saturday, 3 May 1958   *Bromsden Farm*

My father's eightieth birthday lunch passed off pretty well, though Adam was much missed. I think the old boy enjoyed it as much as his depressing temperament will allow him to enjoy anything. I hired a large car with a chauffeur for the day—to get him to my sister's in Hampstead and back—but he never even noticed it!

Diana Cooper flew over from France for the first night of *My Fair Lady* and I saw her briefly.

I hope you got my note confirming the date of the Lit. Soc. as May 13. Alas, I am already hopelessly committed for the evening of the 14th—it's most disappointing. Please thank them very much for asking me: I hope they'll do so again.

I don't know whether I'm a Thackeray fan or not: certainly I'm not strongly agin him. I loved *Vanity Fair* in youth, and *Pendennis* later, and *Esmond* sometime, but I never liked that arch way of taking the reader aside, and treating the characters for the moment as puppets. Some of his journalism is good: I remember 'The Second Funeral of Napoleon', but I never cared for *The Rose and the Ring*, which my father always thrust down our throats. How I should love an opportunity of re-reading W.M.T.'s complete *oeuvre*: how long, oh Lord, how long?

Last Wednesday I took part in a sort of amateur Brains Trust *chez* the British Council. With me were a bookseller and a printer. The audience consisted of nineteen foreign publishers, male and female, black, brown and white, from the Lebanon, Holland, Iceland, the

Sudan and heaven knows where. They all seemed to know English well, and we answered quite good questions for over an hour. Next day the A.P. Herbert Committee on Obscenity had a meeting—and so it goes on.

Oh yes, I must tell you that I have agreed to appear in *The* Brains Trust on B.B.C. Television on the afternoon of Whit Sunday, May 25. I fear I shan't be very good at it, but they pay thirty guineas for an afternoon's work, and it seemed silly to refuse it. Bob Boothby told me the other day that the whole thing is simply a question of practice, and that when you've done it more than two hundred times (as he has) you simply don't notice the cameras at all.

Sunday evening

No interruptions so far, except for seven bullocks which got into the garden. Luckily the ground is so hard that they didn't do much damage. We got rid of them by breaking down a section of fence, cutting two strands of barbed wire, and shooing them through the gap.

Another heavenly day. I mowed all the grass, and then relaxed sleepily in the garden with a manuscript and the Sunday papers. Luckily I don't rely on buses, so the strike ought not to affect me too much. Doubtless taxis will be difficult to find, and goodness knows when some of the staff will get to work. My excellent secretary is leaving at Whitsun: she got married recently: and a new one is starting on Monday. It's a frightful nuisance having to explain everything all over again. And she may be a dud.

Somehow, before I leave for Yorkshire on 6 June, I must contrive to spend an afternoon in the British Museum, and another in their newspaper department near Hendon. I'm also going to compile a full list of all the people, facts and quotations which I still lack for my Wilde footnotes, and circulate it to all and sundry. You must certainly have a copy, just in case something rings a bell. This may not be possible till after my Yorkshire recess. You must forgive my constant harping on Oscar: the whole thing is forever on my mind, and when the book has finally gone to press, I shall feel like a woman delivered of a child, as I did with *Walpole*—a mixture of pride and relief.

Did I tell you that I was unofficially asked whether I'd consider writing the life of Charles Morgan? I said I really didn't think I was qualified, and it would surely be very thin stuff after Hugh—particularly with a widow and two children to be considered. I dare say I shall hear no more of it. The chap who asked me was Lovat Dickson, a director of Macmillan's and a close friend of Charles's. I told him he'd much better write the book himself.

The Briary
8 May 1958   *Eton College*

It is the *man* Thackeray I cannot get to like—hardly any of his letters seem to me at all interesting, and their humour is such fourth-form Victorian (why does he always call his horse his *'oss*—and does 'duty' spelt 'jewty' split *your* sides?). But *V.F.*, *P.*, and *E.* I grant you are *good* but for the button-holing. I expect Dickens was a good deal of a twirp, Forster clearly was dreadful.

On the way to and from Bromsgrove I read and greatly enjoyed Plomer's *At Home*. *Full* of good stuff, and I remember your saying so. My impression that he is a very likeable man was strongly corroborated here by Wilfrid Blunt who knows him (why isn't he in the Lit. Soc.?). I have marked about twenty things in Plomer's book for immortal embalmment (spelling?) in my book (why call it a commonplace book when practically nothing in it is commonplace?). Oliver Van Oss wrote an article about Ruskin in the April *National Review* which had a sentence I think highly of and should like to know if you agree: 'He had the romantic's gift for seeing the inanimate world as if it had that moment left the hand of the Creator'. Jolly good, surely?

'Sir, a cow is a very good animal in a field, but we turn her out of a garden.' We have had bullock trouble too on occasions, and they can do a lot of damage, mainly through blended stupidity and fright (like people). A lot once invaded Luxmoore's garden here, were in it only for ten minutes, but in that time neatly bit out the centre of *every* lettuce. According to the boys, Luxmoore ate nothing but beef for weeks afterwards, till someone told him *no* beef came from milch-cows. How little one knows about such things. A neighbour at Grundisburgh proposed to make a fortune out of selling ten old willows to Gradidge, Gunn and Moore etc., but was disgusted to be told that only a certain kind of willow was any good for bats, and it was not *his* kind.

I am never bored for a moment to hear about your Oscar Wilde researches. Unless the land is on fire when it comes out surely it will have a big sale. I have been told any book about W. is a sure draw, but you know how true that is—or false. I feel pretty sure you were right to refuse to do Charles Morgan. How on earth will all that *dry*ness be made palatable? I don't know his novels at all—except one about a judge which I remember liking, but somehow those Sparken-brokes etc passed me by. Wasn't his reputation abroad *much* higher than in England, and why?

What fun memorial services of beloved relatives are, when there is no tragedy about the passing—and how dear old Hester Alington would have relished the very general pleasure at the meeting of old friends after singing her requiem in Lower Chapel. Some of my con-temporaries do look every bit as decayed and scruffy as no doubt I look to them. One is frequently reminded of that remark of some old peasant-woman in Synge that 'Old age is a poor untidy thing' and of course Winston's reference to 'the surly advance of decrepitude'.

11 May 1958   *Bromsden Farm*

I am writing this at the unaccustomed time of Sunday morning, having only just realised that I should post it to-day if it is to reach you before you leave for London. This afternoon I am to pay a brief visit to a TV-conscious neighbour and watch to-day's Brains Trust: it seems sensible to get some inkling of what I'm in for. I shall post this, short or long, on my way.

Yesterday morning I drove to Oxford, which was looking its loveliest with all its trees green or blossoming. I spent an hour in the Bodleian, looking up Wilde oddments, and then visited Basil Black-well, who agreed to present the London Library with a free copy of every book and periodical he publishes. (I have now visited some thirty-five publishers, and all but one have agreed to do this!)

I am prepared to go all the way with you about Thackeray the *man*, though I shall do so with more conviction after reading Gordon Ray's two vols. Diana's book only came out on Friday, with the satisfactory advance sale of 11,800 copies. Look for my advertisement on the 'Court page' of tomorrow's *Times*. So glad you enjoyed the Plomer book. He is an odd but very likeable chap.

After lunch

I have now done some gardening, read the Sunday papers (very good on Diana) and eaten a huge lunch. My daughter is protestingly mowing the meadow. The hot sun is neutralised almost everywhere by the strong cold wind: clearly what I need is a revolving summer-house!

You're right about Charles Morgan's greater popularity and esteem in France: the same is true of Rosamond Lehmann, and I think perhaps they both have something, in their style and their subject-matter, which translates particularly well into French—though otherwise they have little in common.

I am now re-reading all Wilde's own books and plays, looking for references etc, and most of them are still entertaining. His quip, 'Nowadays all great men have disciples, and it is usually Judas who writes the biography,' was fully borne out by the efforts of Frank Harris and Alfred Douglas. I think you're right in assuming that *any* book about O.W. is off to a flying start: and surely a new book of his own, fuller and more varied than any of his published ones, should cause some stir. Doubtless it will be translated into several languages, though that won't benefit me.

Four weeks to-day I shall be blissfully on my Yorkshire mountain-top. I look forward to this respite from year to year, and about now begin counting the weeks like a schoolboy. Everything up there is almost a month later than it is here, so one has all the fun of seeing a second flowering and burgeoning.

On Tuesday I am going to the dentist at 5, and should be home by 6, but the bus-strike makes the finding of taxis problematical, so it might be better if you came at 6.*15*. You'll simply *have* to come by taxi: the underground during the strike would cause Dante to add another circle to his Inferno. We should get a taxi to the club quite easily at 7. I hope the busmen starve, after slaughtering their shop stewards.

This must be the merest scrap, as I have only just arrived home, there is a meeting this afternoon, and to-morrow is positively costive with mainly tedious chores. Tuesday evening, as always, was most enjoyable; I found to my astonishment that James Smith was once up to me at Eton—which I had totally forgotten and indeed went on forgetting, though I have a dim recollection of a handful of boys serenading me at the end of a half with a glee, madrigal, or catch, which apparently he organised. I *ought* to have remembered it and him. Anthony Powell too was excellent value. You did not, I hope, regard my Philip Sidneyish intention of sitting next to Sir Cuthbert as bogus, but he came in only just in time for the gulls' eggs, and nothing could be done about it. To all appearance he got on extremely well with Jonah. On Wednesday I lunched most agreeably with Ivor Brown and (also as before) found him excellent company. His judgement on men and books seems to me very sound. In return for *A La Carte* he gave me an anthology *England*, edited by himself, shortly coming out, a glance or two at which reveals any number of items well off the beaten track—which is what one would expect.

You would have enjoyed the dinner at my daughter's last night— two absolute charmers, Mrs du Boulay and Mrs Mannheim, both Americans—and are not really nice American women as good and easy company as you could want? One of the husbands after dinner told one of those stories which—well, here you are—A man in a railway-carriage after studying the *Financial Times*, threw it on the floor, exclaiming 'The Stock-Exchange be b—d'! and then saw to his horror that he was not, as. he thought, alone, but that there was an elderly lady in the far corner He apologised profusely, but all she said was, 'I am afraid your wish cannot be granted, as I read this morning that the bottom had fallen out of the market.' Too contrived, I think, but *perhaps* very funny, I simply don't know—Mr Gladstone would not have liked it. Swinburne would, but Watts-Dunton would have checked it as 'going rather too far, Algernon'. Shall I tell it at the G.B.A. meeting in July when the Archbishop is in the chair?

I read *The Stricken Deer*[1] at the Hoods'. Of all unnecessary sources of insanity, is there any more absurd than the fear of everlasting Hellfire? Odd that our ancestors never for a moment realised what utter condemnation the theory establishes of the character of the Creator. Also that eternal torture is impossible. One would get used to it, or go so entirely mad as to be unconscious of it.

But I have no reason to suppose you are at all interested in eternal punishment. Probably you might even refer to the figure of God in a religious picture as Roger Fry did when lecturing to students, viz as 'this important mass'—one of the nice things in Plomer's book.

I never asked about your session at the dentist. Most unimaginative and unsympathetic of me. Fifty years ago I experienced *all* the sensations possible at the dentist's—from the clear, clean flame-like agony of a nerve extracted without *any* anaesthetic to the degraded humiliations of a stump *gouged* out with a sharp spike. Country dentists in the Nineties were medieval in method and callousness. Local anaesthetics—when known, which they often weren't—were regarded as effeminate. The true manliness in the chair was that of Robert Browning in 'Prospice'. 'Let me taste the whole of it, fare like my peers, the heroes of old.' Was that your attitude last Tuesday? I like to think so.

17 *May 1958*   *Bromsden Farm*

Even with our pre-prandial hour, all these Tuesdays seem to flash by before I have said half my say, or you half yours. But may be if we tried to tire the sun with talking, we should tire ourselves first—though I doubt it. Your 'merest scrap' arrived punctually this morning, to my great and accustomed delight. Fancy Jimmy Smith having serenaded you! It reminds me of Anatole France's story *Le Jongleur de Notre Dame*: each man can give only what he has. I duly perceived the good fortune which absolved you from your Cuthbertian

[1] Lord David Cecil's biography of the poet William Cowper.

vow. As you saw, I was weighed down by the inevitable Lockhart, though I managed to talk to dear old Brand most of the time.

What can I tell you? This morning Duff announced by letter that he has changed his mind, and decided he would like to stay at Oxford for two more years. I can only wish him well, and wonder where the hell the money is coming from. He says his decision was largely influenced by his philosophy don, but I suspect it in fact came from his girl-friend, through her parents, who clearly feared that his going down might be the prelude to an early engagement. I don't think they have anything against the boy except his poverty, and I suppose that secretly all parents would like their daughters to marry rich dukes. Did you?

Driven in from the garden by persistent drizzle, I listened to cricket commentaries, from Lord's where Milton was batting, and Chesterfield where Savage was bowling to Johnson (happy conjunction) with Spenser in the slips.

Sunday night

This afternoon, preparing for my ordeal next Sunday, I went to another friend's house and watched my second Brains Trust. It was less dreary than last week's and I am ever so little relieved. My co-Trustees are to be James Fisher, the bird expert; his wife Margery Fisher, of whom I know nothing; and a poetess called Ruth Pitter. *Ora pro nobis!* All depends on what questions we get.

Next week looks like being a hellish rush: into an already crammed engagement-book are bursting Elisabeth Beerbohm and (separately, *bien entendu*) Alistair Cooke. They will both expect time and attention —oh for June 6 and my lodge in the wilderness! Unlike you I am not at heart a social or gregarious person. The fact that I am tolerably good at coping with people is misleading. I much prefer near-solitude, at any rate for long periods. Maybe too much of it would drive me back to the world of men, but I've never had enough leisure to test the theory, and see little chance of it for years to come. So, on with the dance, let joy be unconfined.

One night last week I gave a dinner at the Garrick for Kathleen Coburn, the Coleridge expert, and two other friends. Afterwards we took a taxi to K.C.'s flat for more talk. I told the driver '26 Brunswick

Square,' and he said in a cultured voice: 'Let me see, which one is that? I always get confused between those Hanoverian squares.' And sure enough, he took us to Mecklenburg Square. I thought his remark a curious *trait de moeurs*: one expects New York taxi-drivers (who have no partition between them and their fares) to launch immediately into a discussion on democracy and free will, but in London no such matter. What next?

In Yorkshire, despite the 'Telly', I shall find simpler folk:

> "bright and fierce and fickle is the South,
> And dark and true and tender is the North."[1]

Them's my sentiments exactly, but I daresay it's just the Cockney's longing for rusticity as the annual holiday approaches.

21 May 1958   *Grundisburgh*

It is *almost* blasphemy even to hint that we could tire ourselves with talking. But perhaps I should speak only for myself, and you may be finding it heavy work. I always like to think I am pretty quick at noticing the glassy eye and those little convulsive maxillary spasms which reveal that yawns are being stifled. (John Bailey used to complain bitterly that some physiological perversity made him yawn when in fact he was immensely interested; he thought *inter alia* that it suggested that Providence had a schoolboy sense of humour.) Anyway next Lit. Soc. let it be firmly laid down that I sit next to you. Never mind who is on the other (as Clem Hill said when Victor Trumper died: 'he was the best bat I ever saw, I don't know who was the second'). Lockhart *looks* a bore before he has opened his mouth.

The Strachey book[2] has interesting things, but is on the whole heavyish going, with much repetition. His eulogies are not indiscriminate, but the volume of them tends to make one think they are. L.S. (who somehow was rather repellent, physically) is like those people (I know several) whom one always rather dislikes when they are not there. One does, so to speak, outgrow much of *Eminent*

[1] Tennyson, *The Princess.*

[2] *Lytton Strachey: his Mind and Art* by C.R. Sanders (1957).

Victorians, but last night I took up *Elizabeth and Essex* and by gum! anyone who sneers at his style is surely a fool. Just have *one* look at the description of the Queen in chapter 2 (or 3) and tell me it isn't masterly and I shall get me to a nunnery, and read nothing but Thomas à Kempis. The real flaw in S. is not that he had no religion, but he had no understanding at all of anyone who had; he didn't know what it, or they, meant. How hard it is to tell the truth, and how few do it. I treasure Housman's sentence (omitted from his famous lecture at the last moment): 'Not only is it difficult to know the truth about anything, but to tell the truth when one knows it, to find words that will not obscure or pervert it, is in my experience an exhausting effort.' Sanders says that Mrs Humphry Ward wrote 'an angry letter' to *The Times* about S's essay on Dr Arnold. No doubt she may have been angry (it was a very naughty performance) but her letter was extremely calm and dignified; I remember it well.

I don't think we had any matrimonial feeling about dukes, and I think realised pretty soon that our daughters' plans did not include any special deference to parental hopes and wishes. We trusted their basic good sense, and all turned out well—which does not mean that sometimes we didn't wonder, and still wonder, whether we were not amazingly and undeservedly lucky. Who knows, except God, and He won't say?

That is a very pleasing conjunction of names, though I am afraid it was Herbert Spencer in the slips and not Edmund Spenser. If he is a bowler, he must have discarded the ear-plugs which he used to insert whenever the conversation fell below a certain level. Perhaps he leaves it to the wicket-keeper to hear a snick.

Do you remember the one occasion on which we flatly disagreed? I said that humility was an essential basis of greatness, and you wouldn't have it. In last weeks *T.L.S.* my view has the valuable support of Miss Bogan—of whom I have never heard—and apparently of Yeats. Look at p 268, column 3, line 16 etc, after which, like that prig Brutus, I pause for a reply. And it won't be any good throwing Napoleon at my head, for apparently, according to M. Savant, he must have been the complete man of four letters (the word I hate!). By the same token a good many others are dished too.

You call me 'social and gregarious'. I grant you I never draw breath when in company, but I repudiate 'gregarious'. I flatly refuse almost all cocktail parties and recently the Lady Albemarle who lives not far off told someone she understood I was *a recluse*. Long may she think so. And 'gregarious' from you whose affability to all and sundry is a byword in two continents! Not that I disbelieve you about yourself. Surely no really good and intelligent man is gregarious, or is that too strong? Two or three I have known are certainly bores, and you must know scores. What a costive week threatens. You *can't* have time to write your weekly letter, but what's the good of my talking? I have often urged you not to let it ever be a burden, as of *course* in a really heavy week it must be, but you pay exactly as much attention as Pamela does when I say she mustn't do too much.

Your taxi-driver! The re-grouping of the classes? I heard last week that a markedly 'wet' old boy of mine, whom I had never heard from or of since he left thirty years ago, is now the station-master at Swindon, i.e. the most important junction in S. England! What on earth does one know of anyone?

P.S. If you would like to give real pleasure, send a brief word to old P. Lubbock whose birthday is June 4. He would love it.

Whit Monday, 26 May 1958   *Bromsden Farm*

I am a day late in writing, but yesterday was too crowded, and I may yet succeed in posting this to-day. I am trusting—and hoping indeed—that you didn't see my TV nonsense yesterday. I drove up in the morning to Soho Square, where I changed into one of my less dilapidated suits and had a stiff whiskey. Then walked down to Scott's, where the B.B.C. provided an excellent lunch, rounded off with a man-sized Churchillian cigar. Apart from the producer and his secretary, the company was Ruth Pitter the poet, James Fisher (O.E., KS.) the bird expert, his wife Margery (always known as Angus) and the question-master Norman Fisher, an ex-education officer. They were all charming, and under the influence of food and drink the talk was brisk. Then we were driven to a studio in Hammersmith, where we were clustered together in front of some very bogus-

looking scenery, and given some trial questions (all much more amusing than the real ones later). Then we were made up, more or less;
the ladies in what is called a 'light street', and the men with a few
extra chins painted out, bags under eyes camouflaged and eyebrows
extended. Then back to the studio, with three cameras and two
microphones in action. Blinding lights and much heat therefrom.
Then a terrifying pause, filled with backward counting—'Two
minutes . . . one minute . . . thirty seconds . . . ten seconds . . . Now!'
My mouth became, and remained, as dry as a sand-dune (James
Fisher, who has done it hundreds of times, told me afterwards that his
is always the same). On the whole the questions weren't too bad—
part literary, part ornithological, part general—and the chief difficulty
is in having to give an *immediate* answer. 'Yeats wrote "Too great a
sacrifice can make a stone of the heart". What is the Brains Trust's
opinion of this?' 'What books would you recommend as a picture of
the 1920s?' 'Why are no great hymns written nowadays?' And so on.
After brief reflection one could cook up some sort of an answer, but
out of the blue, under all those hot lights, it's hard—until, I suppose,
one has done it a number of times. Comfort said I looked very nervous
to begin with—as indeed I felt. Goodness knows what the other *three
million* viewers made of it all! Mercifully the number is so large as to
be almost unimaginable. Anyhow I retired the richer by forty-five
guineas, and shall certainly do it again if I am asked—which I very
much doubt.[1]

Afterwards I drove to the Dorchester for a drink with Alistair
Cooke and his wife, who are in London for a few days (I am giving a
little dinner for them at the Garrick tomorrow). Alistair particularly
wanted to meet Ken Tynan whose writing he admires, so I asked him
and his wife to come to the Dorchester too. K.T. is tall and thin, with
long hair and an intermittent stammer. His wife is small, pretty,
American, and recently published a successful first novel called *The
Dud Avocado*. They all got on very well, so at 7 I left them, collected
the car from Soho Square and drove back here, quite exhausted.

How quick of you to spot my Spenserisation of the Leicestershire
player. I'm sure you must have read *Home Life with Herbert Spencer*—

[1] I never was.

a delicious book. I remember particularly enjoying his railway journeys in a specially slung hammock.

I hate to disagree with you, but I'm certain I never denied humility as a necessary ingredient of greatness—quite the contrary, and a search through the 40,000 turgid words of all my letters to you will only confirm this fact. Or do you claim that I made this idiotic remark in conversation? Incidentally, how would you define the difference between pride and vanity? And is humility the opposite or absence of both? You see what effect the Brains Trust is having on me!

I readily withdraw the epithet 'gregarious', realising that, like myself, you are a natural recluse, who talks tremendously when he has to, or feels in the mood. Not that I take your shunning of cocktail parties as evidence: all shun them who are free, white and forty-one.

Tim Nugent is staying with Peter—and playing in the cricket match. He came over for a moment on Saturday. He can't come to the next Lit. Soc., as it clashes with his regimental dinner. I always avoid mine, but then I was merely a temporary and inglorious soldier.

In a fortnight I shall be on my Yorkshire mountain-top. I can't tell you how I welcome the prospect—but first comes the perennial problem of whether I can possibly tidy up everything before I go. And there are several committee meetings intervening—London Library and others—*and* the Fourth of June.

Of course I'll write to Percy L. How good of you to suggest it.

28 May 1958   *Grundisburgh*

Well, God be thanked, Bank Holiday is over. I spent it travelling to Oxford, where on both days the place was positively costive with humanity and traffic and din, and whatever dreams come to the spires must nowadays be mere nightmares. Moreover the proportion of really ugly women in the throng was markedly high (Have you, like me, a strong and definitely personal dislike of ugly women? I can't begin to be tolerant or charitable about them).

We were not within reach of TV on Sunday. I should have liked to hear you, though I can't imagine how *any*one could deal, not only convincingly but at all, with such questions as you mention. Ten minutes' preliminary thought would find me still speechless. It really does sound a pretty grim ordeal, for all the forty-five guineas, and that bumping-race marking of the time. G.K. Chesterton, Shaw, Alington, William Temple are the only men I can think of who could answer immediately and convincingly, but one only heard *them* after they had had much practice. It is interesting to know that Rebecca West (much the cleverest woman in England) is a flop on any Brains Trust—just as the omniscient Lecky after five minutes' agonised thought in that paper-game (all the famous people you can think of whose names begin with H.) is said to have produced Hengist and Horsa and no more. We know, or did know, the two Fishers, a very amiable pair. Your only question I could have answered at all is the one about hymns (why no great ones today?) the answer being that the demand is less, and the existing supplies are ample. Though 'O Valiant Hearts' is as good as any—and many streets better than e.g. 'There is a fountain filled with blood, Drawn from Emmanuel's veins' which M.D. Hill used to say made him feel physically sick (besides being manifestly untrue).

I was staying with friends at Oxford and we had one excellent evening when John Sparrow dined. What good value he is—and, as no doubt you know, he loves the Lit. Soc. Why hasn't he written more? Perhaps the All Souls Wardenship fills his time—but there is nothing of which a Cambridge man knows less than of All Souls.

Who wrote that charming review of Lady Diana's book in the *T.L.S.*? The book has been in the dining-room (a big name for it) here, and I have practically re-read it when P. was away, or late. And I agree more and more with those who praise it highly. I remember your saying once that good reviews have disappointingly little effect on a book's sale, but I have a pleasant feeling—I hope correct—that a good many people *are* reading this, and that the R.H-D coffers are consequently bursting.

Humility. I tried to find the passage last night (this is May 29) but I found that it is impossible to skim your letters—they have to be *read*, so one doesn't get very far in a mere evening. It occurs to me that it may have been, not *greatness*, but *genius* to which you denied humility as an essential element. I will keep you in touch.

Pride and Vanity. Just the sort of distinction I sometimes gave my

73

Extra Studies chaps to worry, and—are you surprised?—A. Huxley, Haldane, Orwell, Connolly, Hart-Davis and Fleming often produced something pretty good. I won't attempt definition (*you* TV Brains Trust chaps can throw one off in a moment) but put it to you that e.g. Milton, like all Puritans according to Macaulay, had invincible pride before men and utter humility before God, that there is no evidence that he was proud about his poetry, but plenty that he was vain about his blindness *not* spoiling his looks; that J. Caesar wasn't a bit proud of straddling the world like a colossus but *was* vain of his looks, and liked the senate's permission to wear the laurel-wreath on his bald head more than all his other honours; that Dizzy was invulnerable to censure or abuse, but it demanded the greatest tact to dissuade him from inflicting his abominable French on the Berlin Conference. But you know lots more.

How right you are about my 'talking tremendously'. After two days at Oxford I practically have clergyman's sore throat. And I *can't* stop. It is terrifying, just as a drunkard or drug-taker *knows* he is killing himself but cannot do a thing about it. My state is even worse, as it is not myself I am killing but my friends. I see nothing for it but a Trappist monastery. And I suspect my letters begin to resemble the young man's description of what he was reading—the young man of Aulla

> who read all the works of Max Muller
> When they asked, 'Are they dull?'
> He replied: 'Very dull'.
> They get duller and duller and duller.

1 June 1958   *Bromsden Farm*

The Glorious First of June has proved wet and dull. The laburnums droop like yellow tears, and the cuckoo calls through a waterfall. Surely my Yorkshire mountain-top will be kinder. Meanwhile we have the Glorious Fourth to splash through, and I suspect only one umbrella among nine (five of us—the first full reunion for almost a year—and four Linklaters). I have a new (off-the-peg) suit for the occasion, very chaste in dark clerical grey, as becomes my age and figure. By the way, all the known 'viewers' agree that the television cameras treated me to a benevolent elongation, so that instead of Holbein's Henry VIII, which they expected, they were served up an old Cavalry Colonel painted by El Greco.

I thought you might enjoy this quotation from Adam's last letter: *plus ça change*: 'During the week I've taken two wickets and made 43 not out, 8 and 50. My window-box is v. flourishing, but in all this gale I've had to stake all my antirrhinums, and it's used most of my pencils.' His cricket must have come on, for, however poor the bowling, one doesn't make 50 without some assiduity and concentration. I swell with vicarious pride.

I so agree about ugly women, though occasionally compassion breaks momentarily through my distaste. Thank God that, with all our disabilities and annoyances, we're not a brace of hideous girls!

I am devoted to Sparrow, but his idleness is not due to the duties of his Wardenship, which are almost non-existent. He suffers (don't we all?) from a delightful congenital idleness, which this post (the plum of all academic jobs in the country) has gently fostered. Almost ever since I have known him (we met as undergraduates in 1926) he has been meditating and preparing a book on Mark Pattison. Did you know that he was a boy-prodigy? He edited Donne's *Devotions* for Cambridge, also Cowley and Bishop King for the Nonesuch Press, soon after he left Winchester.

The *T.L.S.* review of Diana was written by Alan Pryce-Jones.

The reason you can't skim my old letters is that they are, in every sense, unreadable; but the reason you can't find me against humility is not that you have lost some sheets, but rather that I never said it. The discussion must have been with another, or between two quite different men. I hate to think how my early letters must have bored you with complaints of business worries and ill-health. Mercifully the ill-health was entirely caused by the business worries, and ever since Heinemann bought the shares from my friends and relations, both have disappeared. I don't in the least care whether Heinemann's lose their money or not, and ironically, but naturally, my indifference has left me freer for my proper work, and the business has prospered accordingly.

Last Tuesday Comfort and I gave a dinner party at the Garrick for the Alistair Cookes. Peggy Ashcroft came, and it was strange having both my wives at the same table. Peter was there, Rosamond Lehmann and Joe Jackson, the head of Scotland Yard. He was at Piggy Hill's and was a heavyweight boxer. Now for the larks and curlews!

Framingham Chase
Norwich

4 June 1958

Have you ever stayed at a 'Chase'? Do you know what a 'Chase' is? (I don't.) One seems somehow in a Scott-Lever[1]-Trollope atmosphere, and there is even something of Mrs Knox's establishment about it—you remember, a miserable soup in a marvellous old silver tureen followed by a perfect salmon on a cracked kitchen dish. Well here (*chez* Mrs Geoffrey Colman, Pamela's sister) there are trees of primeval age and majesty, a breathtaking blaze of rhododendrons and other flowering shrubs, and flowers so richly and variously coloured that the 'high midsummer pomps'[2] of June can only be seen as an instance of meiosis or even litotes. Very well, but when it comes to writing-paper and envelopes, a good deal of thoughtful research is necessary, and as for pens—well, '*where* is that pen I am sure I saw last week on that table—or perhaps it was the table next door?' (Failure in that quest explains the reappearance of this repulsive Biro.) But it is all very delightful and hospitable, and after all those who originally dwelt in Chases had no truck with pens and paper. Communication with all and sundry was via varlets and scurvy knaves astride of palfreys or stots perhaps of pomely grey, pricking over moor and fen. From where I am writing, I can see cedars of Lebanon that are said to have been planted in the reign of Queen Bess. They make me feel a mere ephemerid, a grasshopper (I speak of the soul rather than of the body). It was Bismarck who always said he preferred trees to men, and in the heart of a Chase like this one sees why—with a great deal of sympathy.

This is the Norwich Festival and this evening we hear Menuhin

---

[1] Charles Lever, Irish novelist (1806–1872).
[2] Matthew Arnold, 'Thyrsis'.

play the Beethoven Concerto, and if you know anything much better than that, kindly tell me what it is. And the B.C. if you please was a 'flop' till Joachim played it! And back to G. to-morrow.

There was what Balfour called 'a frigid and calculated lie' in your letter—no, the epithets don't really apply, but dash it all you said that your early letters to me were unreadable and boring. I have just been re-reading a good many, and they are as full of flavour as a nut or an apple. And arising out of them are several points of moment (1) There are several references to your next visit to Finndale House. Why a' God's name has it never taken place, and is rarely or never now referred to? I suspect you have filled your day impossibly and criminally full and that your nose is a permanent fixture on the grindstone. But please perpend the matter—unless of course you were bored—by no means impossible.

(2) You mentioned two books you would send if I liked them, viz *Abode of Snow* (all about mountaineering) and *The Essential Neville Cardus*. Surely I didn't keep silence, or does it merely show that I was less unblushingly cadging in 1956 than in 1958?

I like to think of you in your northern fastness—its name and whereabouts never breathed by me to any living soul (you remember how Mr Melas shuddered under a similar injunction which, if he disobeyed, 'May the Lord have mercy on *your* soul', and how he disobeyed and escaped by the skin of his teeth, but *not* through anything the Lord did about it).

You are right. Fifty cannot be made with the bat without some skill; wickets can be taken without any—e.g. one taken once at Hagley by the gravedigger, because the batsman couldn't stop a sneeze (hay fever) as the ball was delivered. I like Adam's blend of cricket and horticulture.

John Sparrow. What you say is most interesting. That exhaustion of the precocious happens more often than it should to Wykehamists because frankly they do work their best scholars too hard. They win everything at Oxford and peter out by thirty. But not only at Winchester. Even Raymond Asquith was making *no* mark at the Bar, and told someone not long before the war that he 'found life singularly lacking in motive'. Well, Wellington (the fool of the family), Churchill (who had to cram to get into the army), Birkett (pass degree at Cambridge, I believe) never found it that. And what about your uncle Duff who made so magnificently good?

I took up last week the letters of T.E. Lawrence—which clearly should have been edited by you. You would have eliminated much of that endless jaw about the *Seven Pillars* and his ultimately repellent utterances about its entire worthlessness, which never strike me, at least, as quite sincere. I don't wonder that many of far less venomous spirit than Aldington have been allergic to him, but I expect you have noticed that, like G.B.S., everyone loved him who knew him in person and not only on paper. He had a very wayward literary judgment; has anyone else found *The Odyssey* artificial and third-rate?

That must have been an interesting Alistair Cooke party. Man is of course naturally polygamous, and it is certainly an advance in civilisation that, as often happens today, a divorce leaves the two perfectly friendly afterwards. Byron couldn't do that, but then of course he wasn't quite civilised. He was also extremely stupid not to see that Miss Milbanke was the last wife in the world for him.

I remember old Joe Jackson—a first-rate boxer who lost the heavyweight cup on points because, so rumour said, he didn't like to hit his opponent hard for fear of killing him. Ulysses in *The Odyssey* when fighting the beggar Iras had a similar merciful impulse and instead of killing him with one blow, merely hit him behind the ear so that the surface previously convex became concave. Joe J. refrained even from that. I never knew him, but I doubt if anyone suspected he had detective gifts or tastes.

I say, Rupert, your address in the new O.E.A. books is given as 1 St Michael's Alley!! If this is as it ought to be, my God I have it unto Thee, as T.E. Brown wrote about a much less dreadful happening—death of a child or something.

Does all this bore you? I fear, I greatly fear. You were rather flat about the Max Muller limerick. Probably you knew it.

9 June 1958

The worst of living deliciously in lotos-land is that it *is* always afternoon—in the words of the harassed theatrical landlady, 'Half-past four, and not a po emptied.' I meant to write yesterday, and now I shall have to give this to the nice farmer when he comes up this evening to milk, and if he remembers to post it, you may get it on Wednesday. Blame the delay on to my blessed state of relaxation. I haven't shaved or seen a newspaper since last Thursday, but locusts are plentiful and it looks like a good year for wild honey. Each time I come here I am overwhelmed all over again, first by the beauty of the surroundings, and then by the majestic *silence*. Except for an occasional moor-bird's cry or bleat of distant sheep, there is simply *no sound* from dawn to dusk, and I sit entranced with wonder at this simple fact. You remember the lines about silence coming like a poultice to heal the wounds of sound: well, that is just my state, poulticed, grateful, but not in any way very active. Three glimpses yesterday of a redstart behind the cottage (never seen one up here before) were enough to occupy me for the day. Forgive me if I have said all this before (as from that morbid re-reading you will know): it is a recurrent delight and particularly strong this year.

Your letter was waiting for me in the farmer's house at the bottom of the hill when I arrived on Friday. You shall have *Abode of Snow* when I get back to London, and *The Essential Cardus* too if I can find a copy. Alas, in my ignorance the allusion to Mr Melas is lost on me: please enlighten.

As for 1 St Michael's Alley, I had been hoping to keep that address from you, with its dark hints of contangos, bears and bucket shops, but truth will out, and now you know, or suspect, the worst. In fact the building does also house my father's ultra-respectable stock-broking business, so I must write to the O.E.A. and point out their tactlessness and incompetence.

The last few days before I escaped up here were rackety beyond belief. On Tuesday a London Library committee, followed by a Georgeless Lit. Soc. I just managed to insulate myself against Lockhart by persuading Martin Charteris to sit on one side of me, and

Donald Somervell on the other. The latter told me several anecdotes he'd told me before, including one I'd told him, but made up for it by quoting verbatim (he has a splendid memory) Gibbon's superb footnote on the Giraffe. Jonah said he was against all footnotes, since they simply serve to distract the reader. Having now composed nearly a thousand for Oscar, I felt compelled to disagree. Afterwards Roger came back to Soho Square for a drink, and we then briefly joined my son Duff and his girl in a nearby restaurant. Roger had never met him and wanted to talk about the present state of Worcester College.

Duff stayed the night with me, and next morning we picked up the Linklaters at their hotel (in a friend's car) and drove them to Eton. They were both more than a little apprehensive, Marjorie being theoretically against public schools in general and Eton in particular, Eric feeling the natural *gêne* of a non-Etonian, and neither of them ever having been to the Fourth of June before. By a miracle everything went perfectly: hot sun shone: we immediately joined forces on Agar's with Comfort and Bridget (in our car), found the boys (our Adam and Magnus L.), enjoyed delicious cold chicken and strawberries, brought by Comfort, meeting several Scottish friends of the Linklaters, avoiding all the worst bores etc. The nuisance of Absence[1] etc I avoided by making Duff take the boys in one car, while we escaped (via Maidenhead where we picked up a Linklater daughter) to Monkey Island and an excellent dinner. Parked the cars in Fred Coleridge's drive, enjoyed the fireworks, and I got the Linklaters back to their hotel soon after midnight, exhausted but grateful.

Next day (my last) I desperately tidied up everything, despite interminable intrusions of authors in person, by telephone, in shoals of letters. Lunch with Elisabeth Beerbohm, a long hour with Stephen Potter and the proofs of his new book of nonsense. Then a new committee (at the Arts Council), of which I was reluctantly insinuated into the chair. You shall hear about it next week, for now I hear the farmer's tractor in the distance.

Oscar has come with me in his accustomed bulk. As things stand today I have included 816 letters (long and short), addressed to 206 correspondents. Some will come out before the finish, and I hope a

[1] The Eton name for roll-call.

few will be added, but that is more or less how the final thing will look. I was planning to stay here a full three weeks, but on the *eve* of my leaving I heard that the London Library rating-appeal has been put back to June 30, so I shall tearfully drive south on Tuesday June 24, for conferences etc.

10 June 1958 *Grundisburgh*

Positively celestial mountain book just arrived. I love it, although having a head which gets dizzy on a pair of household steps. But the pictures and descriptions of K2 etc *do something* to me that produces a delicious blend of exaltation and shuddering. It is like having the temperament of a poet with no poetical ability. I am a mute inglorious Whymper.

12 June 1958 *Grundisburgh*

Your letter arrived second post on Wednesday. I was beginning to think my long letter from the Chase had been too much for you. I cannot remember now what topics I brought up, but am sure they must have seemed very dull to you communing with Nature, far away on your Yorkshire wold.

Mr Melas is an example of donnish folly, viz the cryptic allusion. Why should I suppose that you, at least two generations later, should regard the Sherlock Holmes stories as we did in the Nineties? Mr Melas was the Greek Interpreter in the story so called and not a very good one. But will you in return tell me where to find Gibbon on the giraffe—of which I have some dim memory that I once read it, but no more.

Last week we dined with our Bishop and the talk turned to books, and he said he had recently much enjoyed, and had I read, *Old Men Forget*? He said his main impression was what a first-rate chap the author must have been. We saw eye to eye in this matter, and I nearly went on to say: 'But do you know the nephew?' What should I have got. The pursed lip, the raised eyebrow, the sniff, the 'Yes indeed I do'? One never knows; you may have stepped upon some episcopal toe in your time. No more for now, or I may miss the post which reaches you on Saturday.

Kisdon Lodge
Keld

17 June 1958

Your letter duly reached me on Saturday, but this, alas, cannot reach you before Thursday. My kindly farmer, who usually milks his cows up here and posts my letters on his way home, is away for three days' holiday at Morecambe, the cows are temporarily in the valley, and my delicious sloth is stronger than my very real desire to get your letter off on time. Tomorrow I plan to attend a cottage sale near Thirsk, and this will get posted on the way.

I'm sure I love the Sherlock Holmes stories as much as you do, but I certainly don't know them (or their characters' names) half as well. Funnily enough I have in this cottage copies of *The Sign of Four*, *A Study in Scarlet*, *The Memoirs*, and *The Hound of the Baskervilles*—all waiting to be re-read. So, alas, is *How Green*: will you ever forgive me if I don't read it this time? Just now I am in melancholy process of reading through the works of Lord Alfred Douglas: not a very admirable or likeable chap. Altogether I have done quite a lot of work on Oscar, though the end is not yet.

I hadn't time before I left London to look up Gibbon on the Giraffe, but will do so as soon as I get back—in a week's time, alas!—*Lente, lente, currite!*—and let you know. Meanwhile my faulty memory of Donald Somervell's excellent one is that the footnote starts: 'The tallest, gentlest and most useless of the larger mammals. *Camelopardus Maximus*. Little seen in Europe since the Revival of Learning . . .' That last phrase is superb, with its picture of herds of giraffes retreating from a platoon of greybearded scholars.

Did I tell you that my farmer and his family (and their helpless guests) all watched my TV appearance? Such is fame today, though the programme must have profoundly bored and bewildered them, poor things. They are the very nicest people I have ever met, totally unlettered but with superb tact, imagination and good manners.

The frightful new committee which I mentioned in my last letter is trying to create a huge new fund for the advancement and maintenance of literature, authors and the theatre. The money is to come (we hope) from a royalty of 1% on all out-of-copyright books, i.e. those whose authors have been dead more than fifty years. Several publishers have already agreed to pay such a royalty, and it seems *possible* that Stratford and the Old Vic would pay on performances of Shakespeare. At the first 'exploratory' meeting (a dinner-party given by the Society of Authors) Arthur Bryant and I were deputed to see whether the Pilgrim Trust would give the scheme its name and blessing. A.B. and I took Tommy Lascelles out to lunch, and thereafter wrote him a brief memorandum to show his fellow-trustees. They all seemed delighted with the idea, and I then saw Lord Kilmaine, the Secretary of the Trust, who was most encouraging. The Fund's first formal meeting took place at the Arts Council on June 5. Bryant couldn't come, and since I was almost the only person who knew what had happened so far, I was inveigled into the chair. The others present were Kilham Roberts (head of the Society of Authors), Sir William Williams (head of the Arts Council), Allen Lane (head of Penguin Books), Bob Lusty (head of the Hutchinson group of publishers), Rosamond Lehmann, Eric Linklater, Stephen Potter, Lionel Hale, Ivor Brown, and Herbert Agar. Directly I get back I have to see the P.T.'s Lawyers, and all round I can see a pile of work looming. Clearly it's an enormous mistake to take on *any* chairmanship, since one leads to another, and they are all unpaid (not even expenses). If only I could get Oscar to the printer, things would look a little clearer. Diana Cooper's second volume is awaiting my attention, and I shall certainly have to pay a brief visit to Chantilly in July. Up here I just don't think of any of these burdens, but simply laze and Oscarise and sleep and eat—the farmer's wife makes first-class bread and cakes and tarts, with which she is most liberal.

20 June 1958   *Grundisburgh*

What is your eye on in that cottage sale at Thirsk? Pamela would much like to know. She hasn't had much luck lately at sales. Chairs for which her limit is, say, £3.00 go for £17, and once at least the auctioneer ignored her bid and the thing went to the runner-up, an Ipswich dealer, with whom the auctioneer is said to be in unholy league. Like judgment, honesty is fled to brutish beasts. Not that they make much of judgment, if birds count as beasts. A small nameless bird has been in the summer-house for the last ten minutes; and it tries unceasingly to escape through a closed window, ignoring the wide-open door eighteen inches away.

I suppose you *must* read all through Alfred Douglas for O.W's sake. I always think of him as a pitiful figure, for can anything be more pitiful than tragedy without any touch of dignity. And the contrast between that really lovely youth of twenty and the seamed haggard face dominated by that dreadful white and bulbous nose (a really white nose I put it to you is worse than a red one, which, however ugly, is at least suggestive of one-time bonhomie and conviviality, however abused and prolonged). But perhaps A.D. did not see or feel the hideous gap between his promise and his performance. Though are not some of his sonnets very good and (of course) much under-rated? At one time he saw his life's object was:

> To fight with form, to wrestle and to rage
> Till at the last upon the conquered page
> The shadows of created Beauty fall.

Perhaps he thought he had achieved it. He and old Agate used to exchange a good deal of abusive—and amusing—wit from time to time. But I imagine he was pretty detestable most of his life. Poor chap, what could he expect, with that father?

Your whiff of the Camelopardus Maximus has whetted my appetite for the whole passage. What rich *private* enjoyment Gibbon must have got from demure irony. I always suspect there are many instances, especially in the notes, which have escaped notice.

I have just been at the Abbey School Malvern telling the Sixth Form about reading—my gist being largely that they should ignore all damning criticism of old or established authors but not the laudatory, and nearly all of both concerning contemporaries. And that few utterances written or spoken are more fatuous than 'Nobody can afford to miss . . .' and 'Nobody reads X (e.g. Tennyson, Browning, Meredith, Moore) now'. They were a delightful audience ('I dearly love a knot of little misses'[1]). A girls' school, where they don't play hockey and swear, is a very civilised community. Will *you* come and give away our prizes one day? A firm offer. Your journey will be paid for! You would enjoy it more than that awe-inspiring new committee you describe. Why *do* you do these things? From now on you must cultivate the habit of some medieval monastery, where the monks, when summoned by the Abbot to consider and discuss some new proposal, all fell asleep and only woke up when he paused, to say '*Namus, namus*' (i.e. 'we're agin it', short for *Damnamus*) and then fell asleep again. My uncle Edward delightfully likened the Eton staff to these monks, whenever he had some new plan. I don't believe you ever said '*Namus*' to any request (except perhaps to some gushing woman who wanted you to publish her book).

You have, with suspicious carefulness, taken no notice of my reference to your visit here and the possibility of its ever being repeated. I suspect it *is* one of the things to which your attitude is '*Namus*'.

Those serried ranks of booksellers, authors, publishers etc must be immensely hard to get moving: I must resign myself to getting a fortnightly postcard instead of a weekly letter. Meanwhile (1) Stay up north *quam diutissime* (2) Put letter to G.W.L. lower among priorities (3) Practise saying in a deep and throaty voice '*Namus, namus*' every morning (4) Eat plenty more of your farmer's wife's cakes etc.

Kisdon Lodge
Keld

23 *June* 58

Your letter hadn't arrived on Saturday—and I don't wonder, for mine can scarcely have reached you by then. Today I have not stirred from the hilltop, so I shall probably find your letter as I leave to-morrow. This I do with the utmost regret, especially as the weather has improved today, and the evening sun is streaming in on me as I write. The sale last Wednesday was great fun. It took place in a meadow in a little village near Thirsk (about fifty miles away) on the

[1] Doctor Johnson.

85

hottest and sunniest day of my holiday. By great good luck I secured a lovely grandfather clock for £1 (tell Pamela), made in Thirsk and I imagine always housed in the neighbourhood. It stood the journey well (first in the back of my sister's station waggon, and then in a trailer behind my farmer's tractor) and after some days of temperament and the insertion of a few wedges is now ticking away with lulling regularity. I also got an oak chest of drawers with seven drawers and very handsome for 30/-. Also a lovely picture of a sailing ship worked in wool. Such things are usually bought by dealers for several pounds, but this came at the end of the sale, and I got it for 3/-.

I still haven't read *Middlemarch* or *How Green*, being absorbed by Oscar in the daytime, and detective stories at night. I wish I could report Oscar as nearly ready for the printer, but in fact I fear he needs a lot more attention first. I now know so much more than I did when I started (though still not enough) that I keep coming on references in the early letters which now mean something and can be explained. I shall have to read through the whole thing again carefully and chronologically, then write the introductions to the nine parts into which I have divided the book, and try to worry out the more recondite footnotes while the printer is setting up the type—which will take some time. It was of course a crazy job to take on unless one could give one's whole time to it. One should be so soaked in the material that one knows immediately where something comes—and you know how little spare time I usually have. Up here I have been briefly able to concentrate on it, and so get right back into the picture. Luckily I am blessed with the gift of being able to put out of my mind anything that I don't immediately have to think about, so that while I've been here I simply haven't thought *at all* of the publishing business, the London Library, the Lit. Soc., or that new committee. On Wednesday morning, alas, they will all rush back at me, with an enormous pile of unanswered letters on my desk, a morning meeting at the L.L., an afternoon one with Counsel, and so on. Soon Long Leave will be on us, then a visit to Chantilly, but I'm hoping to be able to snatch a few more days up here later in the year. One of my difficulties is that I must most of the time have *all* the relevant Oscariana at hand, and this together with the typescript of the letters, now fills two large cartons. Luckily my farmer is ready to transport anything up and down the hill on his tractor.

There are very few grouse about here this year, but I have seen some snipe, and today for the first time managed to identify one making that drumming noise high in the air. I have often before seen snipe, and heard the noise, but never before been able to bring them together. I haven't shaved since Wednesday last, or seen a paper since Friday's. I hate leaving this beautiful place, the silence, the wonderful air, the ticking grandfather and warm Aladdin lamp, the earth closet, the water fetched in buckets from a spring in the next field, with a high stone wall to climb in between. I have enough books and work here to last me for several months. Newspapers a day or two old, with time to read them slowly, I much prefer to the hurried glance before going downstairs to the office. 'If I ever become a rich man, Or if ever I grow to be old'[1], this is where I shall come. Forgive this elegiac note: my last evening here is always a moving and a mournful time. I realise how immensely lucky I am to have found anything so perfect, but that only makes leaving it the more distressing.

Write next to Bromsden, and on Sunday I will slide back into the accustomed rhythm, with details of my harassed return to the south. Now I must go outside and listen again to the curlews' mournful cry, which echoes my own. As Oscar wrote,

> He who lives more lives than one
> More deaths than one must die.

29 *June 1958*   *Grundisburgh*

Doctors tell one that for one's heart to miss an occasional beat is not serious, so our correspondence will not suffer. I think God did not mean you to write last week, because my letter had not reached you, and you had to write, so to speak, *in vacuo*. Correspondence means the exchange of ideas etc. Some are curiously bad at that and ignore all one's baits. Hester Alington, the very best of women, always thanked affectionately for a letter but made no further reference to it. One was always beginning again.

[1] Belloc, 'The South Country'.

Have you had a long enough holiday? I doubt it. I shall watch narrowly on July 8 to assure myself that you are refreshed in mind and body. We are green with jealousy over your grandfather, and have to be rather firm in resisting the temptation to hope that the time it keeps won't be all that perfect, just as one Forsyte could not help being pleased on hearing that a brother's indigestion lacked some of the mysterious twinges of his own. Bargains are evidently still to be found in the north, but don't forget that Pamela once got a small book-stand *free*—thrown in with something else she bought.

Oscar is becoming your old man of the sea, but I expect you wouldn't not have him on your back. The book should surely have a big sale. How annoying if the human race was wiped out before publication. From the Vansittart extract in the *Daily Telegraph* last Friday the genial Russians about now should be on the move.[1] Poor old Vansittart! How fatal in public life it is to prophesy woe, and then to be proved by events right, up to the hilt. But I suppose he did harp too much on one string. So did Jeremiah; so did Cassandra; so did Dean Inge—and what did *they* get out of it?

We have just had Bernard Fergusson here—to give away the prizes at Woodbridge and talk to the school about leadership, if you please, of all hackneyed speech-day topics. But he was quite excellent and got the perfect blend of *gravitas* and *levitas*, and the whole audience loved it. In proposing a vote of thanks I told them (what is true) that his survival in Burma was really a miracle, and likened the campaign to Camlan where only three of King Arthur's Knights were alive at the end, one because he was so strong that no one dared tackle him, no. 2 so beautiful that no one had the heart to hurt him, and no. 3 so hideous that no one would go near him. Do *you* ever give school prizes away? Beware of answering yes! Some public men are shameless. Lord Evershed, invited in October to come in the following July, answered (roughly) that though his court never *had* sat on a Saturday afternoon, there was no reason why it shouldn't, if it wanted to, and so with great regret etc etc. And I believe he is a very good chap. Old Lawrence, a Trinity oddity, refused a dinner-invitation sent in June

---

[1] The serialization of *The Mist Procession* (1958), the autobiography of the diplomat Lord Vansittart (1881–1957), who all through the 1930s had vainly predicted the German menace.

for the following January 27 on the ground that it was always in that week that he got one of his worst colds.

Your Yorkshire fastness does sound delicious—even the earth closet takes on a cosy friendliness in your description. How dreadful if someone discovered it. I never breathe a word of it. Some day you must read *How Green there*. It would fit—better than *Middlemarch*, which is more attuned to e.g. Woodbridge. Did you have that portentous rain on Thursday night? Almost a record here. For once E. and S.E. England got the worst. A niece of mine is here who lives mainly in Khartum, running the university. She left for leave in April when the thermometer stood at 112 in the shade, shortly after a day on which there were two inches of rain in an hour. All the Egyptians, she tells us, are extremely friendly to the English, that Nasser is not popular, that if we had gone through with the Suez affair, all would have been well, as the Arabs only respect success, etc, and that the Egyptian soldiers strongly resemble the swaggering Scotchman who, after expressing much desire for a battle, ran like a hare when one broke out, and protested, when turned back: 'Mon, they're no fechtin' up yon, they're killin' each ither.'

I am only just home after a visit to one of my girls' schools. The last fortnight in June is costive with prize-days, etc—and next week exam-papers start. I have about 1200, rather more than I desire or deserve and, my God, I shall be sick of adolescent outpourings on Shakespeare before August. You oughtn't really to write at all till *next* Saturday, but I suspect you will, and I shall answer—and I shall send *this* to Soho Square and catch you to-morrow, where alas, after Keld, you will feel your sole communion with nature is to 'watch that little tent of blue, which prisoners call the sky,'[1] if I quote correctly. Who the hell has got my *Ballad*?

29 June 1958   *Bromsden Farm*

This has been a summer's day, and nobody can believe it. I actually got too hot gardening and had to cool off in the shade. What next?

[1] From Oscar Wilde's *Ballad of Reading Gaol*.

My office desk I found piled high, but by Friday evening I was only six letters to the bad. I attended two meetings about the London Library's rating-appeal, which comes on tomorrow morning at 10.30 before the Lands Tribunal in Hanover Square. Both T.S.E. and I have to give evidence, though in fact everything depends on the persuasive oratory of our counsel, Mr Geoffrey Lawrence Q.C. He says the hearing may well last for two days or more, so I fear my correspondence will slip back again. I am going up to London after dinner tonight, so as to get some work done early tomorrow in the office.

I have now finished with the works of Alfred Douglas, thank goodness. Yes, some of his sonnets are indeed good, though not so good as he thought they were. Self-praise, like self-pity, tends to destroy sympathy; all the same:

> To clutch Life's hair, and thrust one naked phrase
> Like a lean knife between the ribs of Time.

are certainly remarkable lines. His tragedy was much longer and less dramatic than Oscar's. He had one son, now I believe in an asylum. I still haven't tracked down the Camelopard, and may have to apply to Donald S. for it.

Of course I'd love to pay you another visit at Grundisburgh, but I don't at the moment see when it is to be. July looks pretty full, and after that I know you are smothered in grandchildren. What about October? This is the one invitation to which in future I shall not, as instructed, answer '*Namus*'.

10.30 p.m. Soho Square

There's a lot to be said for travelling up on Sunday night, rather than Monday morning. There are fewer people on the train (and nobody I know), a smaller queue for taxis, and much less traffic in the streets. The flat seems rather stuffy after the country, but I have opened all the windows and hope for the best. Soon I must con over the evidence I have to give tomorrow: I purposely left it till late, so that it should be fresh in my mind: you shall have an account next week.

We shall have a full house in the country, with Adam home for Long Leave, Duff home from Oxford, and Bridget's young man on leave from the army. As long as I manage to avoid Henley Regatta I shall be content. For a fortnight the town is intolerable, with all possible prices raised—for regulars as well as visitors—you know, all those fat men in tiny pink caps. Why in rowing alone do the old hands have to turn up in fancy dress?

Peter F. is more than half way through his book about the siege of the foreign legations in Peking in 1900, so I should be able to bring it out fairly early next year. He says nobody will want to read it, but I hope he is wrong. About two fields away from Bromsden he has fixed up an automatic gun to keep the pigeons off the kale. Its regular detonations are not what I am used to in the North Riding. Now for my evidence.

2 July 1958   *Grundisburgh*

It is hardly within the bounds of reason, however charitable, that you should desire or deserve another lucubration (I never know what that word means, except that it is faintly derisive) from me, but I send this just to restore our epistolary rhythm, and you will find it in due course at Bromsden.

I see in today's *Daily Telegraph* that you are at this moment in the witness-box (under your full name, which I learn for the first time) with the hopes and good wishes of all good men behind you. I wish I could be optimistic about the result, but I have, like everybody else, become so used, in any and every such case, to see the worse cause vanquish the better that I am full of apprehension. And there is no greater offender than the law, since almost every judge rather sheepishly defends a manifestly unjust law by saying he has no power except to administer it. The oases of civilisation are daily more beset by the sandstorms of barbarism (to write, momentarily, like Vansittart). As I told one of my girls' schools last week, schools are once again, as in the middle-ages monasteries were, the last desperate strongholds of 'sweetness and light,' and warned them that when they go out into the world, they will find most of the standards they have learnt derided or ignored or even actively attacked. A.P.H. battles with fine wrath on your side in last week's *Punch*, but our world is no longer—if it ever was—governed by good sense and magnanimity, and the powers that be, i.e. the cheap Press and the Common Man, are impervious to ridicule.

Have you heard from Percy L. yet? His answer to my birthday letter came yesterday—he always takes some time—and I am sorry to see his eyes have gone back, and he can only dictate. I doubt if he will last much longer, though his letter is not too melancholy. He says his only occupations now are drinking and talking.

I have just begun Belloc's letters and find them rather disappointing. Too much politics and papistry. I read in the preface that H.B. regarded your uncle as the most intelligent man he knew. Why did I never know your uncle? Probably he would merely have thought me one of those pedagogues.

P.S. I see a scientist has said that beer, milk, tea, fried food, early marriage and celibacy all help cancer. And scientists expect us not to think them B.F.'s! *Zu Dienstag.*

5 *July 1958*   *Bromsden Farm*

So glad you like the mountain book: its author[1] is a pet, and I only wish he could write something else. He has had the happy experience of being able always to earn his living by doing what he most enjoyed: after long years in the Indian Army (which were almost all spent surveying in the mountains) he was the first incumbent of the newly founded Chair of Geography at Oxford—a darlin' man if ever there was one.

Adam is home, very tall, spotty and cheerful, for Long Leave, and yesterday we celebrated his fifteenth birthday by giving him a croquet set (much coveted) and laying out a strenuous course in our meadow—which he will now have to mow when he wants a game! Did I tell you that Duff has bought half a car for £17.10.0? I haven't seen it yet, but it is said to be very old, very small, and extremely economical with petrol.

[1] Kenneth Mason.

I had a nice answer from P. Lubbock, very shakily written in pencil.

Sorry you don't like Belloc's letters. I can't help being prejudiced in their favour. I saw a lot of the old boy at Duff's and was very fond and admiring. I can hear his voice in his letters, but I don't think they gain from being read straight through, and are better if dipped into. Oscar's, on the contrary—but you have heard enough of this King Charles's head.

I can hear the distant explosions of the fireworks which signal the end of the Regatta, and am thankful I am not in a dripping punt beset with insects.

The Tribunal was exhausting but fun. It lasted four full days of legal time (10.30–4 with an hour off for lunch) and we probably shan't get the decision for at least a month. (In one way this is quite convenient, since we have the Annual General Meeting later this month, and we shall, Eliot and I, have quite enough to do explaining the raising of the subscription without having to debate the rating question as well.) Our counsel, Geoffrey Lawrence Q.C., was superb, both in his pleading and in his treatment of witnesses. The two opposing counsel seemed like cart-horses matched with a thoroughbred. (Incidentally, one of them, Patrick Browne, a very nice chap *and* a member of the Library!, was at Eton with me.) Lawrence made me the first witness, hoping that I might be able to knock the shine off the ball before Eliot came in. Somehow I scrambled through, but to read the verbatim shorthand account next day was highly chastening. 'Tell me, Mr Hart-Davis', said the rating authority's counsel, 'what is the touchstone by which you distinguish literature from other written matter?' 'How would you define a man of letters?' etc. It was definitely less nerve-racking than the TV Brains Trust, but one always had the feeling that every question concealed a trap. Eliot was terribly nervous, but warmed to his work and finished in fine fettle, rather sorry that he wasn't asked more. (I lunched with him and his wife on Monday and Tuesday. He was most genial and I got him to reminisce entertainingly.) Clearly the judge was entirely on our side, and it is simply a question of the law.

Very hot in the train yesterday, and unfortunately, as I was wearing braces, I could not doff my jacket. Why is it all right to reveal any garment and practically the whole human frame, but never braces? Very odd. *My* braces, at least, have nothing provocative or suggestive about them. Perhaps that elderly man, who finds women with one or no legs more erotically exciting than any others, could throw some light on the matter.

I wanted you to tell me more about Belloc, who from *all* accounts must have been the richest company. What I found disappointing in the letters was—after the politics, which fade away—the enormous amount of space given to descriptions of places he went to abroad. Perhaps many like them, but I always skip them, though, knowing about the writer, I read most of these. And I found the most interesting part of the book was the last, when he could no longer travel and his comments on men and things were full of stuff and had little or no topography. I met him only once at Mrs Cornish's, and of course he was great fun, and incidentally told us that his mother had seen Napoleon after his return from Elba and he looked '*un homme rompu*'.

I am temporarily deprived of the summer-house, as the garden is given over for the day to a platoon of the oldest and most shapeless women in Grundisburgh. How ruthless wives can be when bent upon good works. I shouldn't be in the least surprised to find that the summer-house has been 'tidied', i.e. everything put away in the wrong place or even destroyed ('You *can't* have wanted that filthy old ——' some age-old garment, gadget etc of one's special affection. What ass ever started the notion that women are the sentimental sex?).

I have frequently since seeing you pondered that question they put to you, viz How you distinguish 'literature' from other written matter. I think Housman would have said it was as unanswerable as he said was great poetry—as a rat to a dog. You know it when you meet it, but define it? No.

Lawyers' emphasis on *fact* often obscures *truth*, as it did when Edith Thompson was condemned, when that rather dreadful man Mr Justice Shearman actually interrupted her counsel's address to the jury to underline that they must think of nothing but the facts, and not try to weigh their possible meanings. Has any *good* judge worn a moustache as he did? Or run the hundred yards for Oxford? Sprinters always try to beat the pistol, therefore are essentially unscrupulous and unreliable. The brilliant A.W. Verrall totally failed as a barrister, because he saw through the case he was pleading as clearly as the one he was opposing, and his conscience would not let him conceal the fact. None the less barristers can be first-rate company—also judges, though I was too young to appreciate the wit and wisdom of Mr Justice Wills, who came to Hagley a few years before he made those deplorable observations to and on poor Oscar. I hate them when they moralise and tell the jury they are sure they view the fact that the woman in the dock slept with some man 'with the utmost detestation and horror'. I prefer the perfectly true comment of—who was it?— who when some teetotal ass said he would rather commit adultery than drink a glass of port said 'So would we all, my dear L., so would we all.'

I also wanted to hear you talk about T.S.E.'s reminiscences, in which no doubt D.H. Lawrence and Ezra Pound figured: I bet you got some good stuff—you being one of those to whom people like pouring out. Some day *you* will reminisce, but probably well after I have left for what optimists on patently inadequate grounds insist on calling a better world. I hope you can keep cool in your Soho Square eyrie— which I have never, even in winter, reached not out of breath and perspiring. Equally never have I regretted climbing the steep ascent to heaven. Mid peril toil and pain. Meanwhile cherish the idea of a midweek visit to Finndale in October—often the best of months. But I won't be a bore about it.

P.S. I thought your secretary charming!

13 July 1958   *Bromsden Farm*

Your letter arrived faithfully on Saturday morning, so after a few mishits our long rally is now decorously resumed. Before I forget it, the Gibbon reference is Vol I, Chap IV: the marginal heading reads:

'Commodus displays his skill in the amphitheatre'. Donald had slightly improved the footnote, which in fact reads thus:

> Commodus killed a camelopardalis or Giraffe (Dion. 1. lxxii. p. 1211.), the tallest, the most gentle, and the most useless of the large quadrupeds. This singular animal, a native only of the interior parts of Africa, has not been seen in Europe since the revival of letters; and though M. de Buffon (Hist. Naturelle, tom xiii) has endeavoured to describe, he has not ventured to delineate, the Giraffe.

I discovered that Donald has all his life been accumulating material for an *Anthology of Wit*, and I begged him to let me see some of it. He has a splendid sense of humour and considerable taste, so the result should be good.

I am now slowly, steadily and pleasurably reading straight through (some pages or poems each night in bed) the poetical works of Matthew Arnold, in search of quotations or references quoted by Oscar.

She whom you praised is not my secretary, but my assistant, right hand and great joy these twelve years past. You shall see and hear more of her in due time. Needless to say, your success with her was instantaneous and immense.

We have had a much too busy week-end, in the midst of gales, greyness and heavy rain. Duff and his girl came on Friday. Yesterday Comfort and I dined with the Osbert Lancasters and were persuaded to play bridge till 1. am (we won 2/- each!). This morning Bridget's young man arrived, Mrs and Master Lancaster brought Lucy Moorehead (Alan's wife) over for drinks, and Eric Linklater brought Adam, his own boy and a chauffeur from Eton. Ten to lunch, with no servants, puts a strain on cutlery, china, washers-up. Now they have mercifully all gone, except Bridget and her young man. Comfort retired to bed exhausted after tea. Duff is on his way to six weeks as junior reporter on the *Bolton Evening News*. Last Thursday, in a Junior League match at Eton, Adam took four wickets in four balls! He says the batsmen were useless, but since the last three were all clean bowled, he must at least have been accurate.

I have now got back to the ever-recurring situation in which I haven't room for a single book on any shelf here or in Soho Square. In 1961 Edmund Blunden is due to come home and remove his 7000 volumes from the flat, but what am I to do in the interim? Every day, almost, I acquire some book or books, all duplicates were given away long since, and I have seldom got rid of my only copy of anything without regretting it later. There is no such thing as *enough* books.

Do get H.E. Bates's latest novel (*The Darling Buds of May*) from the library. It made me laugh out loud several times, though I must warn you that Comfort could see nothing funny in it at all.

I must now rewrite someone's manuscript, and I don't feel at all inclined to. I wish more authors were literate and competent.

St Swithin [*15 July*] *1958*   *Grundisburgh*

Thank you for the Gibbon footnote—very rich. Is there any hope of D.S.'s anthology of wit appearing in my lifetime? Do persuade him—and press upon him what is the truth, that he has little to contend with. No one, to my mind, is more disappointing than Daniel George, who seems to have read everything, but I don't find much in his *Peck of Troubles*, *Alphabetical Order*, *Book of Anecdotes*, all being irritatingly just good enough for one to go on reading (which I do every morning in the smallest room) but little more. Though I grant you it is quite possible that, unknown to me, my perceptions and sense of humour are in decline. (Yesterday at a Woodbridge Governors' meeting the question was mooted of getting a retired beak to fill a desperate gap for one term, but he was turned down, because as one Governor said, 'Oh no he's not exactly gaga, but after all he is seventy-two'.)

I am *very* glad that you found no ghastly crisis when you got back on Tuesday after the dinner. I inherit an invincible pessimism, and often feel like James Forsyte who complained, at about my age, that 'the least thing worries me to death'. Luckily Pamela doesn't worry about the same things—or indeed about anything except what affects the family. I often admired the way you kept things going at your end of the table, when you must have been full of nagging wonder as to what it was all about. But that charming lady looked fully equal to the task of ministering angel. I should love to hear all about her; I never saw a face with a livelier understanding.

I didn't know O.W. was fond of Matthew Arnold's poetry. Why have Sitwells etc such a down on him? Percy Lubbock always objected to 'the *vasty* hall of death' in 'Requiescat'. And will 'Self-schooled, self-scanned' etc do in the Shakespeare sonnet? Leavis objects to 'footsteps' in the sonnet, maintaining that footsteps imply movement, which in a mountain is absurd (surely hypercritical?). My *bête noire* is 'Who prop, thou ask'st, in these bad days, my mind?' which challenges Browning's 'Irks care the cropful bird' in 'Rabbi Ben Ezra'. *Per contra* 'Thyrsis' and 'The Scholar Gypsy' are utterly lovely, and why the hell, when I *could* learn, didn't I learn them by heart? And I hope never to read Sohrab's death without that tingle behind the eyeballs, because then I shall be dead in any sense that matters. I rather wish he hadn't given us that simile of Rustum eyeing S. much as a rich lady in bed eyes the 'slavey' (1890) who comes to lay her fire, because surely it diminishes instead of heightening the incident, like the comparison I came across not long ago of the sound of the sea to the swish of feminine skirts, which is to me a good many poles away from

> Black leagues of forest roaring like the sea
> And far lands dim with rain[1]

describing (I think) the view from Luther's Wartburg. I suspect that M.A.'s whiskers and pontifications have a way of inflaming antagonism. Anyway I always resent Dame Sitwell's pedestalling by many, especially when they speak of her facial *beauty*, as to which I content myself with Petrarch's observation about his housekeeper: 'If Helen had looked like her, Troy would still be standing.'

Your *ten* to lunch gives me a headache. On your rest-day too! But how like you are to Florence Nightingale: 'Rest! Rest! Have we not all eternity to rest in?' But is rest restful if you never wake? Socrates said nothing was more enjoyable than dreamless sleep. But not, surely, till you wake up? One often agrees with Macaulay, who thought many of S's dialectical victories were too easy. Perhaps they have often had it out in Elysium.

[1] Quotation untraced.

Your book problem sounds alarming. How like you to house 7000 volumes for someone else. I agree about weeding out. I did that—900 books—when I left Eton for here, and have continually missed any number of them, though they seemed the obvious choice for expulsion at the time. Some were left in Warre House library, but I doubt if any were among the spoils collected by that thief yesterday. I always wondered more thieves did not take advantage of summer afternoons. I always warned boys not to leave money in their clothes. A few heeded the advice but one who brilliantly hid his money in his books was so pleased with his brilliance that he told all his friends about it—and a fortnight later it all vanished. There is always a good deal of thieving, and it is practically impossible to detect, especially as most boys cannot quite remember how much they had. A mad world, i.e. good preparation for the adult one.

20 July 1958   *Bromsden Farm*

It is late at night, and I fear you won't get much of a letter to-day. I always leave Sunday evening, the last of my week-end, free for writing to you, and if anything intervenes there is no time left. This time it was my daughter's second *crise de nerfs*. She has been perfectly happy while her young man has been home on leave, but this evening, as his departure approached, she became very emotional and over-wrought. After Comfort had driven him off to Reading, the poor child broke down, and I had to spend an hour trying to comfort and calm her. Just as her mother did twenty-five years ago, she worries terribly about dying and not believing in God. I tried to persuade her that most people go through something of the same sort, and that when she is happily married and having children she'll be too busy to spend time brooding. She has got a job on the *Farmer's Weekly* in Fleet Street, which starts on August 18, but somehow we must try to fill in her time busily till then—not very easy at a moment's notice, with our own time so occupied. I feel terribly inadequate and ineffectual.

Directly Comfort got back from Reading we had to dispose of a wasps' nest with cyanide: it is in a particularly difficult place, under a concrete path, and I fear we may have muffed it. What next?

Your excellent letter welcomed me on Friday evening. Daniel George is an old friend of mine, but much reading has completely destroyed what powers of selection he ever had, poor chap. His anthologies are mostly deserts of disappointment. One day soon, when I have more time, you shall have a whole letter about the lady you met in my flat—Ruth is her name—and it will all be terribly private and revealing. Meanwhile I am half-way through 'Balder Dead'—not a very enlivening piece, but there are better to come.

Alas, except for the gleaning of a handful of dates, Oscar stands where he stood when I left Yorkshire, and I have now decided that on the four weekday mornings in London I will get up an hour earlier (6.30 instead of 7.30) and devote those extra hours unbrokenly to O.W. I will report progress, if any.

Last week was packed with committees, including that proposed new Fund, which has now been provisionally called the British Trust for Literature and the Arts, God help it. Next Thursday T.S.E. and I must face the assembled members of the London Library at the Annual General Meeting: we had a brief rehearsal last week.

Diana Cooper came in, looking younger and lovelier than ever. She brought a second draft of her second volume, but then took away the third section of it, to be added to, so I can't really get going yet.

All last week the so-called Soho Fair was in operation, with the square made noisy till midnight by the Salvation Army, two or three skiffle groups, thousands of strollers and streams of blocked and hooting drivers. Meanwhile marines and parachutes are piling into Armageddon and Nasser's smile broadens. Pay no attention, my dear George. As you say, we can do nothing, so enjoy your summer-house, and next week I'll try to send you a more interesting letter. I must revert to my old plan of beginning it on Saturday. If only we had any sort of a gardener to do some of the cultivating for us!

24 July 1958   *Grundisburgh*

You have all my sympathy—and so has the young lady. Foolish grown-ups (of whom there are far too many) always talk as if the sorrows of the young are light and transient, and of course to hindsight they may be—like most things—but they are devilish heavy at the time, for the young can't see the silver lining—indeed have insufficient experience to know that there always is one, and *time* weighs so crushingly at that age: 'the years like great black oxen tread the world'.[1] And how disgusting is the discovery that all those damned old saws are true—about work blunting the edge of sorrow, and *tout passe* and the rest of them. The best of all is my old friend Charles Fisher's advice to a hesitating bridge-player (often told to you before): 'Play the card next your thumb.' It is much better advice for life than for bridge. And once you said (kindly) that I never talked like a beak—to which I rejoin sarcastically 'Oh don't I!'

I often find it hard to see why people *should* believe in God, as I once said to Hester Alington. Her answer was that He certainly did make it very difficult, and at such moments one *mustn't worry* but go desperately on—Charles Fisher's line in fact. Much harm—especially to the young—is done by pious folk who pretend that it is all clear and easy and comfy—but as our common friend Carlyle said 'With stupidity and sound digestion a man may front much'.

There is something cheering about your failure with the wasps' nest. That again isn't nearly as easy as one is led to suppose, especially when wasps regard prussic acid as thoroughly toothsome food, as the wasps at Harlech did. Perhaps Celtic wasps are different. Only one year have we had many here, and then a neighbour took forty nests without any visible diminution in the number that made a wasp-line for our jam.

My *internal* pessimism is black and immovable—not mere funk, because I should not greatly mind if I passed away tomorrow, but at the strong possibility that Macbeth was perfectly right in calling life a tale told by an idiot etc. What, except luck, is to prevent three hundred years of painfully acquired civilisation from going up in smoke? But this is vain talk, because a genuine pessimist wouldn't enjoy as I do 'books, and my food, and summer rain'[2] and getting your letters, and writing to you, and dining at the Lit. Soc.—and a day like this, blue and white and fresh etc.

I shall love to hear all about the lady Ruth—as always about

[1] W.B. Yeats, *The Countess Cathleen*.
[2] Stevenson, 'The Celestial Surgeon'.

anything to do with you—and no ex-housemaster, unless he is a fool, is bad at preserving secrets.

'Balder Dead', I remember, tempted one in years gone by to substitute another monosyllable with the same initial. Surely there is nothing in it that could have appealed to Oscar? I am *pro tem* getting up at 6.30 for two hours' paper-marking before breakfast. It is the best time of day, I find.

This is all very small beer, but exam-marking is mentally debilitating. You will be pleased to hear that the Wykehamist entries for the Tennyson paper did contemptibly, and so I said in my report. Westonbirt *per contra* scored very heavily. One boy chose the Lotus-Eaters as his favourite on the grounds of its verbal music—and then produced several lines from a different poem. All the beaks had told their pupils to mention T's onomatopoeia, but unfortunately omitted to tell them how to spell it; one boy wrote it as three separate words. There are some dreadful little beaks about.

Why are you not a life-peer?

27 July 1958   *Bromsden Farm*

Your comments on my daughter's troubles may be beakish, but they are certainly wise, and had you not been so far away (luckily for you) I might have asked you to talk to her: other people's advice is always more acceptable than that of parents. However, the child is apparently recovered and has gone to friends in Wales for the weekend. We find the elder children's comings and goings, with or without friends and always without adequate warning, lead to chronic instability in the larder, which is either empty or laden with uneaten and rotting food. Oh well—you know it all.

My remarks about the wasps must have misled you, for they perished to a wasp!

I like to think that you too have been getting up at 6.30. I did so all last week, finding that first uninterrupted hour a splendid one for work, but disgusted to discover how little I accomplished. Nevertheless the feeling that Oscar is moving, however slowly, is very encouraging, and I shall carry on with the plan.

Last week was a busy one. On Monday I had another meeting with the Queen's solicitor (Sir Leslie Farrer) about that new Trust. On Tuesday I attended a luncheon party in a private room at the Savoy given by W.H. Smith to discuss an annual Literary Prize which they are planning to give. I sat agreeably between Harold Nicolson and Jimmy Smith. Veronica Wedgwood was there and told me that after Lady Rhondda's death it was discovered that she had always run *Time and Tide* on a private account, which was frozen directly she died, so that all the cheques sent to last week's contributors bounced! Nobody yet knows how much the old girl left, or what will happen to the paper. Immediately after lunch I dashed back to the office and conducted a meeting about the Dickens Letters which lasted from 3 till 7. Straight on to a meeting of my bibliographical dining club at the Garrick, where a bookseller friend Percy Muir told me that recently a French bookseller friend of his came over to London and rang Percy up in the country to ask him to lunch in London. Percy explained that he couldn't because it was the day of his village fête. Asked what this meant, Percy described the stalls, bowling for a pig etc, to which the Frenchman replied: '*Ah, oui, en France on appelle ça un garden party.*'

On Wednesday I spent most of the morning going through the proofs of Stephen Potter's new (and ostensibly funny) book with him—an exhausting job. In the evening Comfort arrived for two days' holiday in London. We had an excellent Soho dinner and went to a delightful French musical called *Irma La Douce*, all about sex.

On Thursday I lunched at the Garrick with one of the directors of Macmillan's, who formally invited me, on behalf of the firm, the family and the executors, to write the biography of Charles Morgan. After some discussion I went so far as to say that I would *consider* the possibility on condition that I could take all the papers home, that I had a completely free hand, without family vetoes, that there were no fixed dates for beginning or ending the book (goodness knows when I could start or how long it would take) and (most important of all) that they succeed in finding some way of paying £500 a year for three years, either to my two sons or to Eton and Oxford, in the form of covenants or a trust fund, so that I pay no tax on it. I thought this would put paid to the invitation, but my friend took everything in his stride, and promised to consult lawyers and accountants. Certainly such an arrangement would take a load of worry off me, but then the book would have to be written! It wouldn't be half as rich and amusing as Hugh: there isn't the same material: but it would be an immense challenge, to which all my literary longings might well respond. We shall see.

After this momentous lunch I hurried to the London Library for the Annual General Meeting, which was attended by 150 or more members. T.S.E. led off mellifluously, and then we swapped chairs, and for almost an hour and a half I stood up answering questions—an exhausting process, and for the first time in my life I had recourse to the water on the table. However, all went well in the end, all resolutions were carried, and the subscription was raised from six guineas to ten. The rating verdict is to be delivered next Tuesday at 2.30: I shall attend the court to hear it.

Then, still Thursday, I took Comfort to a cocktail party given by Patrick Browne (our O.E. opponent in the rating-appeal) and on to a long exciting film about the war in the Western Desert called *Ice Cold in Alex*. We both enjoyed it, but I was all in when we got back to the flat.

Except for Boothby, the new Life Peers are a pretty dim lot, and the whole thing seems to me quite pointless.

Do you know the novels of Rumer Godden? Many of them are excellent, and I recommend the latest, *The Greengage Summer*: if you like that I'll tell you which others to try.

At any moment I am to meet an American journalist, aged ninety-nine, who interviewed Oscar in the Middle West in 1882: he's sure to be gaga, but one never knows.

31 July 1958   *Grundisburgh*

I am black with sympathetic rage[1], though I suspect you expected it. I did, merely seeing the thing from outside and knowing that in these squalid times when financial interests are opposing those that are clearly civilised, the former always win. All good men know what

[1] At the failure of the London Library appeal.

ought to be done and I am sure the P.M. is among them. But if he proposes to take the burden off the London Library all the asses opposite will at once object 'then why not off the Hoxton Lending Library?' Damn them all! The invariable outcome of this conflict is one of the proofs that we are in for a new Dark Age.

> The signal-fires of warning
> They blaze, but none regard;
> And on through night to morning
> The world runs ruinward.[1]

But no more of that; I suspect that you are just as impatient of my gloom as my family are. And Cassandra was murdered, and no doubt Jeremiah was too, though history is silent on the matter. A large percentage of old men tend, as the years pass, more and more to resemble James Forsyte: how good Galsworthy was in that tale, though it is practically blasphemy to say so nowadays. Mere photography they sneer. Well I prefer a good photograph to a portrait in which all the tones and colours are largely arbitrary. Does anyone really think that in fifty years the *Saga* won't be valued more highly than e.g. *Mrs Dalloway*? Bah!. *The Man of Property* was one of the books set in the Certificate exam, and I have just been reading a good deal of callow and mainly second-hand judgments on the Forsytes. It is the literary criticisms, never the factual answers, which make one almost suicidal with boredom and irritation—and knowing that 2/20 is really the right mark for practically all and that one must not give it. Anyway I am nearly through now, and have not committed suicide yet—even after perusing the script of Miss Betjeman (daughter of John?) who wrote *forty-eight* sides on her five answers, not solely through that cerebral diarrhoea which she shares with nearly all schoolgirls in the G.C.E., but from having so enormous a handwriting that three and sometimes two words a line affronted one's eye. And all the candidates at her school (St Mary's Wantage) had the same sky-sign writing, and their bundle of eighteen scripts felt and looked as if it contained at least forty. I will send you a specimen page if I can.

'Chronic instability in the larder.' A pleasing phrase. Don't I

[1] A.E. Housman, *More Poems*, XLIII.

know it! The only answer is a permanent ham in the fridge, for, as C.M. Wells always says, 'All hams are good, though great hams are very rare; there was that one at Bembridge in 1899, and Allcock's at Aberdovey in 1904 and ...'. They totted up to about eight in all. Incidentally C.M.W. invariably calls Allcock '*Nil Nisi*' or sometimes 'Nothing But', having in his make-up an engagingly fourth-form strand, the other strands being great, but I suppose not imaginative, scholarship and a profound knowledge of moths, wine, and salmon-fishing—plus of course cricket and football, though he rarely speaks of either, except that when primed with Hermitage he will tell a first-rate story or two about Tom Wass or Abel, or even tell you of his best innings, viz nine runs on a ruined and crumbling pitch, in the dark, against Richardson and Lockwood—and of course no protector. 'I needn't have had a bat; I was hit all over from chin to heel, but I didn't get out that night. I was bowled first ball next day.' By Tom Richardson, whose genial way it was to say as his victim passed him pavilion-wards: 'Best one I've bowled this year, sir.' All old cricketers of any aesthetic sense will tell you that Tom R bowling in 1894–8 was the finest sight in the world. And he committed suicide—like Shrewsbury, Stoddart, Albert Trott, A.E. Relf and many others. I wonder why. 'Sir, you *may* wonder.' As so often, Dr Johnson provides the only answer.

Did you, do you, have the same matutinal technique as mine? Up at 6.30, cold sponge of face, brew a potkin of tea, work two hours, then bath, dress, breakfast? And have you noticed how often the mornings, 6.30–8.30, have been bright and sunny, whatever horrors may follow? I am sorry about Peter's hay, I really am. It is the shadow over so many of my summers—the sight of ruined or spoilt harvests, hay or corn. So far, not much damage has happened in Suffolk—we get much less rain than you do, and only a few fields between here and Ipswich are tousled—just as if they hadn't brushed their hair—not laid flat. Nature is a tremendous ass, besides being quite inartistic, as O.W. said.

I haven't read a single novel by Godden—in truth hadn't even heard of him!—and I find to my shame that the Ipswich library is full of them—so I have taken out two, *The House by the Sea* and *The City and the Wave*. Are they what you recommend? Let me know, because in spite of your morbid taste for Brussels sprouts, I still have confidence in your judgment.

That is *most* interesting about you and Charles M. But have you, shall you ever have, the time? It will be grand if it comes off, because of course you ought to be writing. Though C.M. must be less fun to write about than H.W. There will be a lot of reading to be done too, including those rebarbative novels—not that I did not enjoy one or two very much. He seems to have been a curiously unpopular man (that appeals to you, I know) and I suppose conceited. Still, his comments on life and letters were very often, *me judice*, of first-class value. He was probably great fun when tight. But was he ever tight? Anyhow, good luck to you. But a' God's name don't fill your plate too full. I look forward to hearing how it all goes.

It is a gorgeous day here, and shortly I leave the summer-house for lunch, where I shall have beans and bacon (the *de rigueur* dish at all Worcestershire *archery* meetings in the early Nineties. Have you kept up your archery, as Roger Ascham insisted?) and raspberries and cream, and anyone who wants a better lunch than that can whistle for it—he won't get it.

(After lunch)

Just what I expected. I can just tolerate your liking for sprouts, but if you said you *didn't* like the broad bean, the matter would take a graver turn. It is true Pamela is *not* sound on this matter, but of course there is the compensation that thereby *I* get more of them. And what is your attitude about spinach? I used to hate it but don't now. All depends on the cooking, and with *cream*! Don't I recall that that was one of the items on old Heythorp's dinner? The book is indoors. It was nice to find that you were far from being averse to gastronomy.

4 August 1958   *Bromsden Farm*

I am so geared to the two-day week-end that a three-day one throws me out: by messing about at the beginning I end by achieving less than in the ordinary two days. I didn't write last night because, knowing I had today up my sleeve, I was finishing the typescript of

Peter's new book, *The Siege at Peking*, which he unexpectedly brought on Saturday, eager for an immediate (and reassuring) verdict. This I was luckily able to give, for I found the story absorbing and excellently told. I doubt whether many younger than you, except for a few sinologues, know anything at all of the Siege of the Legations— I certainly didn't—and he has told it without tedium anywhere. Today I have been struggling with a huge book on Havelock Ellis (the centenary of his birth falls on 2 February 59) by my old friend Arthur Calder-Marshall.

Comfort and Adam have just (8.45 pm) returned exhausted from a regatta. Adam won nothing, though he got into one final and one semi-final. He says the prizes were rotten anyhow—'useless things like ashtrays'. Once again he missed a Distinction in Trials by 43 marks, but secured the Science Prize (ugh!) for C. Next half he tackles the G.C.E. Will you correct any of his papers? I fancy he won't make much showing in English.

I see Cattley is dead: I never knew him to speak to, but didn't much like what I heard about him, though Duff found him helpful in the School Library. I'm sure he was a suppressed paederast—how say you?

Do you realise that your last splendid letter was six quarto pages long? You must have been delirious with relief after correcting all those frightful essays. The Betjemans live at Wantage, so clearly the young elephantographer is our Mr B's daughter.

My 6.30 a.m. ritual is simpler than yours. There is only an hour for work, since I have to start the day proper at 7.30, so I sit straight down to it, without wash or tea, and stumble on till they ring the Angelus in St Patrick's church across the square—and that naturally is the moment when I have just, at last, got something moving.

We all went to the Lands Tribunal to hear the old fool deliver his judgment, which he read from a typescript, haltingly and with a thick but soft brogue which made hearing difficult. This appeal has cost the Library well over £2000, and I can't think there's much point in our spending even more to hear the same miserable points of law argued before three judges in the Court of Appeal: however we are to have a meeting with Lawrence next week, at which all will be decided. I expect you saw that excellent leader in *The Times*: it was written by A.P. Ryan, who told me next day that he knows both the P.M. and the Chancellor are concerned at the plight of the Library, and that was why he mentioned them so pointedly. The subsequent letters were all much to the point. I think the next move is a public appeal for money (letter in *The Times*): apart from the legal costs, we now owe the Revenue some £12,000 of arrears, incurred while our appeals have dragged along. E.M. Forster (now seventy-nine) wrote a charming letter, offering a donation of sixty guineas.

It also looks, alas, as if that other Trust is going to materialise: the Pilgrim Trust have voted up to £500 for its foundation expenses, and Tommy Lascelles told me privily on the telephone that, when the new Trust is in being, the P.T. will almost certainly make another 'substantial' grant if asked. I see more work and committees looming.

Rumer Godden is a woman, but the two books you mention are by her sister and quite outside my recommendation.

Of course I like broad beans: in fact I like almost all food except various branches of offal—and I might even like them if I didn't know what they were. I love liver and kidneys, so why should I be repelled by the thought of heart, head, brains and trotters? I particularly like spinach in all its manifestations.

Last Friday I hired a car and drove to Roehampton, where I had a brief interview with the Roman Catholic Archbishop of Southern Rhodesia. How do you explain that, my dear Holmes? During the week I also went to a theatre, and dined out three times—once at Greenwich.

Now I must scramble out 250 words on my author 'Elephant Bill' who died last week. And there are 'blurbs' to be written for the catalogue, and Havelock Ellis is still lingering in his twenties. Next week, as I always hope, you shall get something worth reading.

7 August 1958   *Grundisburgh*

Put in the way you do, i.e. six quarto pages, it is clearly well beyond a joke, elephantography in fact—a beautiful word. My old friend Tom Cattley never wrote more than a side and a half octavo for the simple reason, which he often gave, that he had nothing at all in his head; he had plenty thirty years ago, but even then he was no great talker, and his normal temperature, literally, was 92, which may account for a lot. You are quite right; like many bachelor beaks—many of them excellent beaks—he was a sublimated homosexual, the adjective, or rather participle, being just as certain as the noun. He was perhaps a little too frank in his preference for bright boys of fourteen to all boys, bright or not, of eighteen. The result of which was that he didn't make much of his house, and his old boys had little feeling for him.

I am glad Peter's Peking book looks promising. I remember all the fuss half a century ago but none of the details. In those happy days we knew we were secure enough, and anything that dimly affected our interests could be put right by a couple of English gunboats just showing themselves. And not only were we much happier, but everyone else was too. I have read a few of the articles in Peter's last book and found them very lively, e.g. his career in the O.T.C. at Eton. Lately in the *Spectator* he has struck me as a little tired, but my impression may be wrong. What on earth are *you* doing with Havelock Ellis? Not that I know anything of him but a few pages of some immensely serious, and important, and unreadable tome on sexual aberrations, but though I am sure the subject has the most absorbing and hilarious possibilities, somehow I went no further. Was he a very good man? Malcolm Muggeridge says somewhere, when asked (probably by Kingsmill) if he would have liked to be Shelley, that he 'would rather be Streicher or even Havelock Ellis', but I don't know why. You will be able to tell me.

A science prize sounds very impressive. I never got within sight of one. I once won a history prize, and still have the Globe *Boswell* Arthur Benson gave me—a better prize than the good conduct prize I won in 1895 at Evelyn's, which was called *Among the Holy Places* with a lot of steel-engravings of the dullest imaginable places in Palestine. *But* it was bound in tree-calf, so, like any other thirteen-year old, I treasured it as a thing of beauty. I may see Adam's Eng. Lit. papers next December; one can never be sure. He will pass all right.

So far *all* the letters I have seen about the London Library have been on your side. What about that one which seemed to make it clear that the letter of the law was *not* binding on the Tribunal, however much the Chairman seemed to think it was. Mind you badger the P.M. about it. Even now the right thing does occasionally happen.

How the devil is one to know that the Christian name Rumer is feminine? It isn't a name at all. And you didn't tell me which books of Rumer I should read. I didn't make much of her sister's two books, but there is a whole shelf of Goddens in the library, and they can't all be by her sister.

I am glad you are sound on beans. I don't think I have tasted trotters or head (calf's?). Brains I rather like in small quantities. You are not, I hope, repelled by sweetbread. Your gastronomic tastes are as catholic as were old Saintsbury's literary ones. He must have been before your day, but no doubt you know some polymath, though in these hurrying times the breed must be rarer. Are you going over to Rome—or emigrating to Southern Rhodesia? What did that cryptic sentence mean? How, when your diary, i.e. letters to me, is published, will the editor explain it? I think of interpolating a malicious note to the effect that you had been much impressed by the miracles of St Januarius. Did you know that Thomas More was canonised only recently, the long delay being because Catholics resented his light-hearted remarks on the scaffold. Like the Germans in 1914, who said the English were worthless and frivolous people because they sang 'Tipperary' before battle.

I have been reading Hardy's life by his widow—very interesting, though she misses numberless opportunities of being more interesting. If only it had been written by Hugh Walpole's biographer! One gets very fond of the old chap, so calm and wise and unassuming. Is E. Blunden's life of him good? I don't think I have read it.

What shall I answer first? Havelock Ellis was an immensely hand-some but impotent ninny, who wrote many books in dull and often clumsy English. Because of his impotence, shyness, high squeaky voice etc, he accepted as normal *all* forms of sexual aberration and, as you know, wrote a multi-volumed work on them. This was prosecuted and banned in England: the attendant publicity caused all the sexual misfits of the world to write to Ellis, and he gradually became their prophet, healer and guide. He married a Lesbian who gradually went off her head. He lived to be eighty. There's much more to him than that, but maybe you'll read the biography next year: it is very frank.

Duff has been awarded a 'major County Scholarship'—size as yet unknown. Perhaps I told you this last week. Anyhow Duff celebrated by taking all ten wickets for 29 in a Bank Holiday match in Wales!

We're no forrader with the London Library, since our Counsel was away all last week, sitting as Recorder of Chichester.

Rumer Godden's best books are *Black Narcissus, A Fugue in Time, An Episode of Sparrows, The River* and the last one, *The Greengage Summer*. If you find nothing in any of these I absolve you from further effort.

I love sweetbread: I wonder who brilliantly coined that name to obscure the physiological truth?

I journeyed to see that Archbishop to ask him to release Christopher Devlin (now a Jesuit missionary in Southern Rhodesia) so that he can come home for a year or two and write *the* biography of Gerard Manley Hopkins for the Oxford University Press. My friend Humphry House had written a lot of the biography when he died, and as his literary executor I am anxious that his work should not be wasted. The Archbishop was wearing lovely purple socks. He told me a great deal about his difficulties in S. Rhodesia, but listened sympathetically to my plea, and said he certainly would not stand in the way of the plan. The next move is with the Jesuits, to whom I have reported. It would be a great relief to get rid of this responsibility.

Those two volumes were not in fact written by Mrs Hardy, but by old T.H. himself. All she did was to put them together. E.B.'s book on T.H. is wayward in construction but full of curious information and critical acumen.

Last week began, mercifully, on Tuesday, when an old friend, Douglas Grant (a Scot, now Prof of Eng. Lit. at Toronto) came for the night on his way back to Canada. I took him to dine at the Travellers' (the Garrick being shut for holidays) and after dinner we sat with

Alan Pryce-Jones and Tony Powell. Alan was most amusing about a phenomenal fortune-teller he recently consulted. Without knowing even Alan's name this chap told him that he'd had an uncle who committed suicide (which happened twenty years ago) and other astonishing exactitudes. Then he gave the chap three letters in separate, blank, envelopes. Without opening them the chap described the writers with extraordinary skill.

On Wednesday I lunched with James Laver and his wife (very old friends) in their beautiful new flat in the Boltons. Next to me was Harriet Cohen, a wreck of a woman, full of stories of Sibelius, Paderewski, Elgar, Arnold Bennett, all of whom thought her the cat's whiskers, as no doubt she was. That evening I dined with a Canadian woman-professor from the West Indies, who is editing Coleridge's *The Friend*. Next day lunch with a Swiss professor from Geneva who has just published a thesis on *George Moore et La France*. Then visits from an Englishman called Cavaliero, who has been teaching in Malta, and a French professor from Lille who is compiling a bibliography of Beckford. Babel, my dear George, from which I was quite glad to escape to a meeting at the Arts Council about that new Trust. A.P.H. has now joined the party (of which I am still reluctantly in the chair) and he suggested calling it the Phoenix Trust, which we may well do if it's possible.

I didn't much like what little I knew of Brendan Bracken, and in the only near-business relation we had he carted me good and proper. Louis Golding[1] I first met at the Drinkwaters' in 1930. Then he was a brilliant talker, but the success of *Magnolia Street* turned his head and he became a bore. I once incurred his wrath by telling a mutual friend, with some reason, that I didn't consider Louis a suitable person to go to a boys' camp.

University Arms Hotel
Cambridge

13 August 1958

If the H. Ellis biography has much in it like the brilliant (and revealing) vignette of him in your letter, it will be a best-seller. 'A

[1] He and Bracken had recently died.

handsome but impotent ninny' ought to be copyright. I shall certainly read the biography.

I suppose old Hardy wasn't enough of an egoist to write good autobiography; and possibly he didn't think anything said by Shaw and Galsworthy at lunch was worth recording. I enjoyed E. Blunden's book greatly (just read it; didn't know it was here), his judgments are never superficial or commonplace. And I am now in the middle of *The Dynasts*, last read at Cambridge I think. It is tremendous. I should have thought even the critics of the day could have seen that.

That fortune-teller sounds most impressive—no chance, I assume, of collusion or preparation. All worlds on either side of death will be open to us some day, which may be the Almighty's way of dealing with the menace of over-population of the earth (if indeed He cares twopence about the earth—you see the impact of *The Dynasts*!). What He clearly is *not* bothering about is the Grundisburgh harvest; the last week has been almost entirely fine but for *just* enough rain every twenty-four hours to stop any harvest work. As an old farmer said to me grimly last week 'Thirty minutes' rain may easily cost a farmer £300'. Why don't we buy *all* our cereals and devote ourselves to supplying the world with meat? Don't answer; of course there is a snag somewhere.

An old pupil, Rex Whitworth, has just written the life of some great but unknown general.[1] Harold Nicolson gave it quite a good review in the *Observer*. But had H.N. his tongue in his cheek when he said R.W. had the graceful style one would expect from an ex-president of 'Pop'? Or does he think 'Pop' is what it was in old Gladstone's day? I have known many presidents who were practically incapable of speech. (*I* was once president—and did one good thing, viz got Alec Cadogan in while still in a scug cap. There had been growing up a belief that some colour was essential to membership—like that adolescent 'Philatelic' at Harrow.)

I never met Brendan B. But his utterances on and to the Governing Bodies Association committee seemed to me very apt and refreshing, though undiplomatically expressed. 'The whole plan, to my judgment, is completely imbecile' was one of the most recent—and I am bound to say an opinion I was strongly inclined to agree with.

[1] *Field Marshal Earl Ligonier* (1958).

Dr John Murray is another who makes it quite clear that he considers nearly all proposals about education to be off the target. He is one of those trenchant blends of Scottish and Oxford. I first met him in Charles Fisher's rooms (*circa* 1906) where, when asked his opinion of William Temple's *Christian Philosophy*, he put the book in its place as being by a man who was 'neither a Christian nor a philosopher'.

I imagine B.B. could be pretty awful. One can't tell much from obituaries. Oliver Baldwin was full of silliness, egotism, *un*-divine discontent, contempt for others (and of course for authority, discipline, tradition etc).[1] He was at Macnaghten's (who Barrie said was one of the best men he had ever met) and, like other failure Etonians, made no effort to get the good out of the place, but expected everything to be done *for* him, and never stopped picking holes and grizzling. Latterly, they tell me, he was addicted to the bottle, and that he was homo, but I know nothing of that. His fellow-soldiers found him so intolerable that whatever course might be going which took a subaltern away from his regiment for some weeks, O.B. was always sent on it, not, as no doubt his aunts thought, because of his mental brilliance. But he must have had *some* good stuff in him, though he never really gave it a chance. What a mess a little folly and conceit can make of a man's life.

I like your discreet and demure remark about Louis Golding and the boys' camp. I have forgotten *Magnolia Street*. Can a writer make a fortune now as he used to, e.g. *If Winter Comes, Economic Consequences of the Peace, How Green was my Valley* etc? George Trevelyan told Claude Elliott that his *Social History* sold I don't know how many copies but brought him only £3000. The trend, I suppose, when half England belongs to a party which frankly hates anyone to be prosperous by his own efforts and not by their damned enactments.

I have brought away with me *Black Narcissus* and *A Fugue in Time* to read in the intervals of evaluating the portentous outpourings of Miss Betjeman.

Looked in at Heffer's Bookshop. It is a *very* swell affair compared with what it was in my day. The man *we* knew as Young Heffer in 1903 and congratulated, to his obvious pleasure, on his really extraordinary resemblance to W.B. Yeats, died a few years ago. He was

[1] Elder son of the Prime Minister. He had just died.

very absurd but cannot have been at all a fool as it was in his day the shop went ahead by leaps and bounds. Monty James used to complain of his prices for secondhand books and often got the book he wanted from old David's stall for a—comparative—song.

I am always particularly delighted at seeing a gummed-up letter of yours, for it generally means that you have reopened it to add a juicy tidbit, and this last one is no exception. I loved your praise of *The Dynasts*, which I am sure is T.H.'s masterpiece.

I never knew Oliver Baldwin, and never heard a good word said of him: your remark about 'courses' in the Army brought it all back to me: one could often keep an undesirable officer almost permanently away on some course or other: a messing course was considered the nadir. I was lucky and spent only one week on a course in five years: it was on Aircraft Recognition, and took place in a desolate mansion outside Dorking. I found Macaulay's *History* in its library and read him delightedly each evening after our nasty dinner. At the end of the week I could distinguish almost any plane from any angle, but since they mostly became obsolete in a matter of months, *cui bono*?

I think it's still possible for a writer to make a fortune out of one book, but it more usually comes from one play or one film.

Last week was comparatively peaceful, since I had reserved two days for visiting the Arthur Ransomes in Lancashire; they couldn't have me, and I spent one afternoon in the B.M., and one in the London Library, footnote-hunting for Oscar.

I had another meeting with Geoffrey Lawrence, at which we decided to carry the London Library's case on to the Court of Appeal (though this is secret until the committee ratifies the decision on September 9). I'm sure this is the right thing to do, for reasons too complicated for enclosure here, but to be told you when we meet.

Did I tell you that my secretary (who had only been with me three months and wasn't very good) never returned from the August Bank Holiday? Her father rang up next day to say she had collapsed under the strain, and for the past fortnight I have been struggling with half-witted and ignorant temporaries. Yesterday I engaged a seemingly charming and well-qualified girl, who will report for duty when I get back on September 4. The nuisance of having—for the third time in a year—to explain everybody's name and address etc etc is scarcely supportable.

And now, as promised, and very much for your eye alone, I shall briefly tell you about my darling Ruth. She is a little older than I am, her maiden name was Ware, and she was brought up in Hereford-shire, where her father was a choleric and impoverished man of leisure who captained the county in the Minor Counties champion-ship. When she was nineteen she went up to London and got a job with a Jewish printer called Oliver Simon, a very good and successful typographer and printer of fine editions. He fell in love with her, proposed, and out of a mixture of being flattered and feeling grown-up she accepted him. She was never in the least in love with him: he had a fearful inferiority complex and a nervous grin: his mother was a Rothenstein (sister of Will) and they all came from Bradford. They had two children, who are charming. The marriage staggered on unhappily.

I must now switch to Comfort. She is one of the (I suspect) many women whose sex instincts are in fact wholly directed to the produc-tion of children, and when their quiver is full they want no more (as they say in the courts) intercourse. So it was with her: when we married in 1933 she was passionate and gay, but after Adam's con-ception in 1942 she had had enough. I bore this enforced chastity uneasily for four years: if I had been a person who could flit from flower to flower, that might have provided a solution: but I am not: sex to me is indissolubly linked with love. And then in 1946 I met Ruth, and we fell in love like steel-filings rushing to a magnet. It was touch and go whether we didn't elope immediately, but somehow we held on, for our families' sake. I told Comfort about it, and she took it wonderfully, saying she was rather relieved on the sexual side, but hoped I wouldn't break up the family. I said I wouldn't. Ruth told her husband, who preferred to play the ostrich and go on pretending he knew nothing. Soon after this I got Ruth into my business, where she has been my prop and right hand ever since. For twelve years now we have been lovers in every sense, always blissfully happy together, with a complete unity of interests and of stillness. We are together in the office, in my flat whenever possible, and best of all in Yorkshire. We first visited that neighbourhood in 1947, and have been thereabouts every year since, but it wasn't till 1954 that we found the ruined cottage which we have restored and christened Kisdon Lodge. It had had sheep in it for fifty years, so in its new incarnation it is our creation, our child—the one place we can be quite alone.

I would have told you all this years ago, but first I thought you might be shocked, and then the opportunity never seemed to come. Two years ago Ruth's husband died, which made her life much easier. Now her children have left home, and one is married.

Sometimes we wonder whether our love has been fostered by all our difficulties, and then we think that perhaps it must be very strong to surmount so much. What the end will be I don't know, but on Tuesday we set off for another blessed fortnight. I wrote most of *Hugh Walpole* in Yorkshire, with R. typing each page as I finished it, and criticising brilliantly. Comfort is so used to the set-up that it is seldom mentioned. Sometimes she is unhappy, I fear, but I can find no better solution.

20 *August 1958*   *University Arms Hotel*

I am much honoured and touched by the story you tell in your last. It is, you know, something like an idyll—like the Book of Ruth! I mean of course objectively, because to you it is much more than that. Nothing was ever truer than *Amor vincit omnia* (as Chaucer's Prioress, in whose company I have been for a week, wore on her brooch) and both *Amor* and *vincit* have a score of meanings, from the depths to the heights—as indeed *omnia* does too. There really is something triumphant in what you tell me and in the way you have handled an immeasurably difficult situation—made so by the Immanent Will, which so often and so disastrously allows the union between this man and that woman, which seemed so promising, to be harmed, and it may be ruined, by deep and unforseen and unmendable discrepancies. Shocked!! I can't think you really thought I might be that. (Though I dislike those—often young women—who proclaim that they are

118

'unshockable'.) But I only by what strikes me forcibly as vulgar or mean or cruel, none of which elements remotely enter the love-story of Rupert and Ruth. Please let me meet her again some day soon—by which date you will (probably) have been able to convince her that I am less old and hidebound and slow-witted than I look—or at least that all the good wishes my heart holds for you shall always include her too.

The 'awarding' is nearly over, and I return home on Thursday. This hotel is comfortable, and to me there are few purer pleasures than living off the fat of the land for several days at someone else's expense. It is of course far too hot, as there are many Americans here, and I have for *five* nights slept under a sheet and nought else. Have you ever noticed how curiously ugly all middle-aged women who frequent hotels are? One exception here—a young Greek maiden who my susceptible colleagues insist must have been in Homer's mind when he imagined Nausicaa. The other women at her table must be the spit of the Queen of the Laestrygonians, whom he described in one unforgettable vivid line, viz: 'She was as large as a mountain, and when they saw her, they hated her.'

Drawbacks? (1) My pillow is too bulky, and I wake with a stiff neck. (2) The man next door snores—one of those reverberating snores like thunder among the hills. (3) The wine-waiter has bubukles on his nose, and my erudite confrères address him as Bardolph. (4) I left my sponge in the bathroom, and it has gone. I think of putting up a notice like that one at the Athenaeum 'Will the clergyman who stole my umbrella kindly return it. This club consists half of gentlemen and half of clergymen, and it is clear that no gentleman would steal an umbrella.' For 'clergyman' read in this instance 'American.'

I am sorry L.A.G. Strong is dead: I met him once and liked him. He married Brinton's second daughter, a nice girl. Wasn't he rather a good story-teller?

I have to be very tactful and reticent these days, as you will understand when I tell you that the livelier of my colleagues thinks *The Dynasts* 'dull stuff', *The Irish R.M.* moderately funny, Carlyle and Meredith intolerable, H. James an old humbug, has never heard of *Earlham*—and hates porridge. *Per contra* he thinks Max B. the greatest writer that ever lived and Tommy Beecham the greatest conductor. Another, when D.H. Lawrence is denigrated, behaves rather like Dr Arnold when St Paul was by someone put above St John. 'He burst into tears and begged that the subject might never again be mentioned in his presence'—so Arthur Benson tells it.

Kisdon Lodge

25 August 1958
Keld

You've no idea what pleasure your letter gave us both. I knew you'd see the point, but you did so in a particularly wholehearted and delightful way. Bless you. I fancy the period during which I thought you might be shocked must have been brief, and after that I hesitated for fear of appearing unnecessarily disloyal to Comfort. She is a wholly *good* person—no vice in her at all, unselfish, uncomplaining, hard-working, but also now utterly unsentimental, with her deeper feelings so submerged as to be unguessable. Mercifully this teaching occupies and to a certain extent satisfies her. Enough of that.

This place is indeed for us the Earthly Paradise. Except for our beloved farmer who comes up the hill each evening to milk his cows, bringing our letters and yesterday's papers, we are completely by ourselves, in the most beautiful place imaginable, without machines or noise of any kind. I can't remember how much I've told you about the cottage (I think if you looked back at my old letters you'd find I'd never lied about the situation here, but simply prevaricated by avoiding mention of Ruth). Anyhow it consists of two rooms, one above the other, each with a tiny room opening off it. The bedroom is wide and low, with a miraculous view, and is furnished (as is the sitting-room) entirely from local sales. (I first thought of bringing *your* clock here, but it suited the flat so well that I had to leave it there, and now we have our splendid grandfather here.) The sitting-room also contains two comfortable arm-chairs, four other chairs, a wide kitchen table, and a superb desk-bookcase-chest-of-drawers (£1 at a sale). A splendid old range-fire downstairs, and a little coal one upstairs, which we light every night, for the luxury and pure pleasure of it. The tiny downstairs room is a combined pantry-kitchen-larder, in which we had a sink installed. All the water we fetch in buckets from a spring in the next field. We wash in a basin by the fire.

The cottage is in a green field and surrounded by others, with the wild fell starting one field above. Outside we have a coal-shed and E.C., with flagged paths leading to them. When we first arrived, these paths were buried under a fifty-year growth of turf, and it was the greatest fun unearthing them. All the buildings are made of local grey stone, as are the walls between fields, and all the farmhouses in the dale. We also have a porch with an outer front door. This acts as a wind-break, and contains a stone bench and our garden chairs and table. We eat out whenever it's nice enough—which hasn't been often this past week. In fact the rain, which looks like ruining the farmers by leaving bumper crops of hay to rot ungathered, has proved a blessing to poor old Oscar and his editor. I am going through all the letters and notes chronologically, preparing them for the printer, and Ruth is retyping each batch of notes as I finish it. So far I have done three and a quarter of the nine parts, and the possibility of concentrating on the book, with *no* interruptions, makes all the difference. Ruth is also staining the bedroom floor, painting the E.C. door etc, so we are busy at something all the time. Thursday is my (fifty-first) birthday, and we shall celebrate by going to a sale in a nearby village.

Duff writes in jubilation to say that his piece about his trip to West Africa on a cargo boat has been accepted by *Blackwood's*. No word from Comfort and Adam in Scotland, but I expect they'll write for my birthday.

I loved your account of the Cambridge hotel. Whenever I travel at the firm's expense I always enjoy the luxuries enormously, but I'm completely happy only *here*, where everything is slow and simple and primitive. From the bookshelf *How Green* looks reproachfully down, but, at risk of your taking umbrage, I am ignoring its blandishments and sticking to Oscar: this is my one chance of getting a clear run at him.

When we have to go shopping—usually to Hawes in Wensleydale, eight miles away over a steep pass—we pack all our purchases into haversacks and carry them up the hill. It's a precipitous twenty-minute climb up a rough track: only a tractor or a jeep can manage it on wheels. We have Ruth's little car here, a tiny Renault, which we leave by the road at the bottom. Write here this week, and then alas to Bromsden. We plan to drive south on Wednesday September 3. It takes a good eight hours, but we are now so used to it that we take it easy and don't let it tire us unduly. Ruth is longing to see you again: perhaps before the October Lit. Soc.? I had known L.A.G. Strong for twenty-five years and liked him very much. Not a wildly exciting chap, but genuine, generous, businesslike and kind. I think he was a good storyteller, but I suspect that, like so many, he exhausted all he had to say quite early on, but couldn't stop writing. Latterly I saw him always at the Royal Literary Fund meetings. Are you swarming with grandchildren? I only hope the summer-house is inviolate.

27 *August 1958*   *Grundisburgh*

Good! Do you know this correspondence has got so woven into the texture of my life that I was quite depressed at Tuesday not fulfilling its normal role of red-letter day of the week. And when the first post on Wednesday could produce nothing but a note from my banker denying the possession of a share certificate which I distinctly remember sending him, I very nearly phoned crossly to my Cambridge hotel saying they hadn't posted a most important letter I put in their box last week. I inherit an abiding pessimism about such (and other) things from my father. And somehow his defence, viz that if you always expect the worst, all the surprises you get in life are pleasant ones, like all other philosophical theories, ought to be more reassuring than it is. One or two things said by old James Forsyte always remind me of him, e.g. J.F.'s gloom about his cellar after his death: his excellent claret 'would be spoilt or drunk, he shouldn't wonder'. Surely that 'or drunk' is a delicious touch. Not that my father ever took his wine seriously—or anybody else's. I never remember the Hagley claret having the chill taken off it, and I am sure he meant eulogy when he said of our extravagantly insipid port that 'it would do nobody any harm'. Like so many of that generation he got his wine from some old friend on the verge of bankruptcy. Old Austen-Leigh of Eton similarly used to produce a wine which Walter Durnford said tasted like corked quinine. The beaks of the Nineties didn't know much about teaching, but by gum they had character. There are fewer such every year in every walk of life. And anyone of my age understands less and less what is going on. I humbly bought a paperback novel recently of which *eight* million copies have been sold, and beyond a certain rude vigour could see little or nothing in it. *God's Little Acre*[1] it was called. I found no character of the smallest interest. That is always happening to me. But I liked the two Rumer Goddens you mentioned, especially *Black Narcissus*. She has a great feeling for houses and their personalities. I shall embark on others of hers, when the flow of exam-papers from Barbados ceases, i.e. in another ten days or so—and then I have papers to set for next year. August and September are my (only) working months.

Kisdon Lodge as described by you makes my mouth water, but I want a little pen-picture of the 'miraculous' view. Is it moor and fen or crag and torrent? And what in the way of *trees*—of which, like a fool, I learnt nothing when I was young, and now when it is too late I love them increasingly, as that old ruffian Bismarck did, though I don't yet, as he did, like them much better than human beings. Of course he knew mainly Germans.

At Cambridge I won a bet of a million pounds. A dogmatic exam-colleague, with whom I saw the *Titanic* film, said that the tune of 'Nearer My God to Thee' was by Sullivan. I said it wasn't, and when he said 'What will you bet!' I said 'A million pounds', being really quite sure, but not really wanting to take the pound off him that I know he would have bet (an excellent but cocksure fellow). Of course it is by Dykes, as so many of those honeyed tunes are which we all pretend to be superior to, but really enjoy. I was once nearly complained of at Eton when in 'Lead Kindly Light' my spirited shot at a high E in the tenor part didn't quite make it, and the soulless beak in desk resented the sympathetic but undeniably hearty laughter of my neighbours. Luckily my tutor was Arthur Benson.

Your Duff is clearly marked out for a littérateur. Don't let him write like Amis, Leavis, Hovis or anyone called Wilson. All your offspring are bursting with brains, as one might expect. Have they their father's awe-inspiring energy too? Very doubtful. Who has?

[1] By Erskine Caldwell.

28 August

You will be sorry to hear that I have discovered a clear case of cribbing in two Certificate papers from British Guiana. My reporting of it to H.Q. will probably lead to war, or at least a demand for independence. The prize up to date is divided between Macbeth to the ghost 'Never shake thy curly head at me' and on the same occasion, 'Thou canst not say it was me who done it'. Another bright lad wrote that Lady M. said that if she had a child like M. she would 'pluck my nibble (sic) from his boneless gums'.

You must some day read *How Green* at Kisdon Lodge. It is made for it. Does your Ruth know it? Because if it isn't a *beautiful* book—an adjective *never* to be used unless one is sure of one's ground—I will become a Trappist monk and live in perfect silence on beans.

I look forward greatly to seeing Ruth (cheek!) again. You have no doubt warned her that retired schoolmasters are a pretty uninteresting lot, but I am encouraged by the thought that she is sure to like the people *you* like. And sometimes I feel defiant, like the Night Watchman[1] (I quote from memory) 'Lots o' people have made the mistake of thinking I was stupider than I was'—pause, then 'stupider than what I looked'—another pause, then 'stupider than what they thought I looked'. A divine man. And his name was George!

Kisdon Lodge

Keld

31 August 1958

Your tale of a blank Tuesday was so pitiful that somehow I must try and get this to you on time. If I give it to my farmer tonight, and he remembers to post it, all should be well. I am sitting on the flagstones outside the cottage door in the *sun*, which has shone deliciously yesterday and today. Sunday or no Sunday, I can see farmers and their wives and families haymaking in a dozen fields far away—but you want the view described, and I should have to be a combination of Ruskin and Wordsworth to do it any kind of justice.

Swaledale is a broad green valley running pretty well east and west for some thirty miles, from Richmond to Keld, which is the end

[1] The narrator in many of the short stories of W.W. Jacobs.

of Swaledale proper, or rather its beginning, for it is here that the River Swale first takes shape and name, fed by many mountain streams and waterfalls of great beauty. As one drives up the dale from Richmond the scenery grows gradually wilder, and here there are only very green grass fields up to where the brown-green of the fells begins towards the top of the surrounding hills. The cottage is high on one side of this wide green valley, 1600 feet above the road, on which even the twice-daily bus and an occasional lorry 'show scarce so gross as beetles'.[1] Behind us, one big field away, the fell begins. We can see as many as a dozen scattered farms, all built of the same local stone as the field-dividing walls. Cattle and sheep are the farmers' livelihood. The sheep are on the fells except in the depth of winter. A proportion of each farmer's fields is permanent pasture, and the rest kept for the hay on which the animals live in the winter. The only change ever in the look of the fields is their turning various shades of yellow-green as the hay ripens and is cut. The word 'fields' needs qualifying, since few of them are flat and many precipitous: their contours and varieties on the opposite hillside are a constant source of joy, particularly when the evening shadows deepen the ghylls and hollows with mystery and beauty. We are some way above the tree-line, and all the hilltops which stretch one beyond another in all four directions are bare and noble. Some way below us, straight down, there is a charming wood of ash and birch and hazel, but that is invisible from here. Along the road are to be seen occasional tall elms and other umbrageous trees. The tiny village of Keld can just be seen to our right at the bottom. Straight ahead the furthest range to be seen (about four away) is in Westmorland, near Kirkby Stephen.

Yesterday, for shopping, we drove north, over the most desolate and beautiful moors imaginable, to Barnard Castle on the Tees, and home by Richmond. Both B.C. and R. are charming towns. Have you a good map of the neighbourhood?

As it is Sunday, Ruth is frying us some sausages, bacon, tomatoes and potatoes for lunch. Usually we have a cold lunch, and always boiled eggs for our supper. The farmer's wife bakes us endless delicious cakes etc.

---

[1] *King Lear*, Act IV, Scene 6.

Later. The clouds have now rolled up, and I am continuing this indoors, while Ruth re-plasters the inside of our little built-in cupboard (the cottage walls are at least three foot thick).

I am sure your opinion of *God's Little Acre* would be mine, and that the eight million are fools. A sale of that size should have made you suspicious.

Ruth is thrilled by your messages and longs to write to you herself, but I have restrained her: *someone* must do the manual work. How nice to find you quoting the Night Watchman: I was brought up on him, and have most of the books, but haven't looked at them for ages. I had forgotten that his name was George.

Every day here I have worked at Oscar, and am now on the sixth of the nine parts. Here are a few of his jokes, from the time when he was reviewing books for the *Pall Mall Gazette*:

Andiatoroctè is the title of a volume of poems by the Rev. Clarence Walworth, of Albany, N.Y. It is a word borrowed from the Indians, and should, we think, be returned to them as soon as possible.

K.E.V.'s little volume is a series of poems on the Saints. Each poem is preceded by a brief biography of the Saint it celebrates—which is a very necessary precaution, as few of them ever existed . . . Such lines as those on St Stephen may be said to add another horror to martyrdom. Still it is a thoroughly well-intentioned book and eminently suitable for invalids.

Judges, like the criminal classes, have their lighter moments, and it was probably in one of his happiest and, certainly, in one of his most careless moods that Mr Justice Denman conceived the idea of putting the early history of Rome into doggerel verse for the benefit of a little boy of the name of Jack. . . . If Jack goes to the bad, Mr Justice Denman will have much to answer for.

Perhaps you knew them already. None of them comes into my book, but nevertheless I shall be surprised if the massive volume does not amuse, move and delight you. I wonder how long it will be before I am able to enjoy it objectively, without thought of dating or cross-reference: years, I expect.

If tomorrow is fine and sunny we are planning to drive forty miles to Morecambe or its attendant watering-place Grange-over-Sands, and bathe in the sea. We have never been to either place, and we have a great affection for such North-Country holiday resorts, provided they don't lose their heads like Blackpool. Tuesday will be Oscar here, and the sadness of packing the cottage up for the winter; and on Wednesday we shall drive weeping south. I shudder at the thought of my office desk piled two-foot-deep in letters and manuscripts demanding attention. My new secretary reports for duty on Thursday: I hope to goodness she's efficient.

Ruth has arranged lovely bouquets of wildflowers all over the cottage—she always does—and they will have to be sadly committed to the flames before we leave. I've had a cheerful letter from Comfort in Scotland, where the weather seems to have been better than here. Write to Bromsden, and from among the litter of unpaid bills and uncut grass I will answer.

4 September 1958   Grundisburgh

I have got your picture of Swaledale (a delicious name). Excellent! Ruskin would have had at least half-a-dozen lines of blank verse. The K.L. view seems to have everything—in water and hill, and far horizons, and all the colours there are, shifting with the movement of sun and clouds—not out of range, I hope, of nice farm-noises and sheepbells, but no hedge-crickets, I suppose, or redbreast whistling from a garden-croft. This is the time of year, when, believe it or not, the robin comes and sits on the mowing-machine as I mow (but I don't do much mowing now). Ornithologists say that it is the Nazi of the small bird world, a ruthless bully and monstrously selfish. Nature is no sentimentalist, and didn't mind giving the little villain what a grandchild calls that lovely 'orange chest'.

Now, my dear Rupert, perpend. The next Lit. Soc. is on October 14. I stay with my daughter Diana for it. She is here now and wants you to dine on *either* the 15th or the 16th and of course your lady-wife too if available, but I think you said she never is in mid-week. Pamela too almost certainly won't be there. I know your soul is entirely above such things, but you will get a very good dinner and as good a cigar as Havana can put out when on its day. The fact that you will have seen me on the 14th and heard all my conversation, though slightly daunting I admit, must not put you off. Remember your Horace: '*Nihil est ab omni parte beatum*' or, *anglice*, every silver lining has its cloud. But Diana and her good man much want to meet you (neither has *any* intention of writing a book).

You have never told me whether you read in bed. Probably not, as you must always be exhausted by 12.0. But let me tell you that as a bedside book Jacobs's omnibus volumes (there are two) are unsurpassed. Each story is of the right length, and you fall asleep chuckling, which is better than any barbiturate. *The Irish R.M.* is of course another. And—as who knows better than you—stuff as good as that does not get staled by age. So many people *tick* books off like American tourists in Rome.

I am glad to hear Oscar goes well. I like the three gems you send. So many writers since (e.g. Guedalla) have attempted his brand of wit that it seems to me quite likely that our sillier critics may be deceived into thinking that anyone can bring it off, that it is *vieux jeu* etc. But surely the book must be a best-seller? Do you know at all when it will be out? Don't wait until the tastes of the common man (damn his bleary and myopic eyes) have infected all readers. And a' God's name don't forget I am 75⅔.

Morecambe I saw once on a Bank Holiday—an obviously lovely spot made into a small hell by *homo sapiens* in astronomical numbers and holiday mood. I fear that you may not have found it much better than Blackpool, which is simply and frankly HELL. Tuppy and I once visited it in August. You literally couldn't see any sand, there was so solid a crowd on it; and there were some six mechanical bands along the front playing fortissimo different tunes. The silver lining to the nuclear cloud sent over England by the Chinese will be that nothing will be left of Blackpool, and beyond that colossal wreck only will 'the lone and level sands stretch far away'.[1]

P.S. I don't believe Sonia C's story[2] of that game with King Edward—sliding bread and butter pieces, butter downwards, down his trousers

[1] Shelley, 'Ozymandias'.
[2] From *Edwardian Daughter* (1958) by Sonia Cubitt, née Keppel.

—not once but often. I mean, he may have been a fool about many things, but surely not about trousers?

Here I am again, back to the treadmill, the noise, the interruptions —and the sweet routine of writing to you on Sunday evening. Thursday was fine and sunny for our long drive: we left at noon and reached Soho Square at 9.30 p.m. London seemed—indeed was— terribly noisy and stuffy after our cool and silent mountain-top. Moreover, as you will have read, the next day (Friday) was a London record for heat and humidity: I was in the Henley train when the thunderstorm broke. Here everything is drenched and dripping, and our lawn is rather like William Plomer's. He wrote the other day from his Sussex bungalow: 'Our lawnette, when stepped upon, closes over the ankles with a noise like gargling, and squirts jets of water up one's leg.' Comfort says the kitchen garden is full of interesting pond-life, never seen there before—but we have masses of ripe and ripening *strawberries*! Apparently a late variety and most acceptable, since we haven't a single plum, and the remaining apples are steadily being beaten from the trees. Too wet for mowing, thank goodness, and I have pulled Oscar on to 1898.

You ask about farm-noises at Kisdon Lodge. On still days one can hear lowing, bleating and barking from the dale and the opposite slope, and on still nights the rushing of the river below. In August the immediate noises (curlew, lark, plover, grouse) are far fewer than in June, but there were still some. Did I tell you that on one of our last days we picked a jam-jar-full of wild raspberries just down the hill? Lots of harebells still, and wild geranium, loosestrife, ragwort etc, with heather, bilberries and rowan berries—oh I am so homesick for it all, and shall remain so until next June.

I sent you a postcard this morning, saying I'd love to dine with Diana on October 15: I shall much look forward to the evening. And you'll be at Soho Square at six on the 14th, won't you, to see Ruth again.

Yes, I always read in bed, but usually sleep swiftly overtakes me.

Detective stories I generally read, but I see that it's time W.W. Jacobs had a turn. There are some dozen volumes of his in my bedroom here, so that is easily arranged. But I am still in course of reading through *Aurora Leigh* and Matthew Arnold and Oscar's other favourites, in the hopes of running to earth a few more of his quotations, so my bedside table is piled high.

Oh yes—our drive to the sea was a great success. We reached Morecambe about 1. pm, the high tide was slapping the orange-peel up against the foot of the promenade, and we immediately saw that bathing there was not for us. So we bought a picnic lunch and drove on another twenty miles to Grange-over-Sands, on the other side of the bay. It's a wholly charming little place, like a bit of Cheltenham set down between hills and sea. We had a delicious swim off some rocks, ate our lunch, and drove home *via* Kendal, where we had tea and visited the tiny secondhand bookshop. The sun shone intermittently all day, and strongly in the evening, so that our drive home, through Sedbergh and Wensleydale, was beautiful beyond words. We shall go to Grange again one day.

Comfort came back cheerful and sunburnt from Scotland; Adam returns on Tuesday; Duff has retired to a caravan in Wales to work for Greats. His County Scholarship is for £200 a year: isn't it splendid! Particularly since the Charles Morgan project has now evaporated. His widow has decided that she doesn't want any mention of his love-affairs, and wants to postpone the biography for twenty years. This seems rather hard on Charles, since by then most of the people who knew him will be dead, and I can't imagine why this decision wasn't reached before they asked me to write the book. However, except financially, I'm rather relieved, and perhaps I'll find something better to do instead. They say (Macmillan's) that they're thinking of bringing out a volume of Charles's letters.[1]

My office desk is piled high with letters from everyone I've ever heard of, all waiting to be answered. My new secretary seems calm and efficient, so by the end of next week I should be up to date. Next Tuesday the London Library committee meet, I hope to endorse my intention of taking our case to the Court of Appeal: you shall have a

[1] *Selected Letters of Charles Morgan*, edited with a memoir by Eiluned Lewis (1967).

full report next Sunday. Later this month I have to fulfil an old engagement to speak at the Library Association's dinner at Brighton. To my horror I have just discovered that it's white tie and decorations, which will mean an expensive visit to Moss Bros, since my old tail coat and other accoutrements are all too old, tight and shabby. What a nuisance!

Now I must advance into 1899, and then spend a few minutes with the Night Watchman.

10 September 1958   *Grundisburgh*

Excellent! October 15. You have probably had the invitation by now. Diana is generally pretty quick off the mark. I don't know who she is going to get. Probably someone they think you don't know, and whom it will turn out you have known for years. On the 14th Alexander (I forget whether D. goes too) will be back from India, after a fortnight's stay there, and what we hope will be a successful effort to save India from bankruptcy.

I feel deeply for you—leaving Keld and arriving in London with its (almost) billion mud-coloured inhabitants. I like W. Plomer's description of his lawnette under water uttering the sound which must have begotten the Suffolk word 'stolchy' for muddy. Your *strawberries* fill me with envy. Have they *any* flavour? (cattish!) I also envy you your Kisdon noises. Once we could counter with a watch of nightingales ('ollerin away all night' as a disgusted rustic put it), but building operations have ousted them, and now the bulbul is as rare as the hoopoe.

Aurora Leigh I read at Cambridge but can't remember a word of it. Arnold Bennett, in one of those *Evening Standard* articles bringing culture to *hoi polloi*, recommended it, and that old ass Ruskin said it was 'the greatest poem in the English language'. Perhaps you will tell me you agree—even after coming across the passage in which 'daunting' rhymes with 'mountain'. Did Oscar really read it? It is very unlike *Reading Gaol*.

All my papers from Barbados have now arrived, and I shall be shot of them in three days. How intolerably *wordy* young women are on paper; they keep on saying that someone is brave and courageous, or humble and modest. But they *absorb* the set book like sponges, and would score full marks if they could write English. And they are always capable of such things as I got this morning: 'Lady Macbeth said she knew what it was to snatch her baby from her boneless gums and dash it on the ground.' And of course *all* say that Macbeth was 'very annoyed' to see the ghost (or 'goast'; after all we have 'toast') in his chair. They have all been told to quote Goethe; and so they do, but under some pseudonym like 'Geotha' which puts that majestic old goose among the Anglo-Saxons with Hroswitha etc.

You keep a brave face about Morecambe, but admit you drove on for twenty miles. I was at Grange once with Tuppy and recollect nothing beyond that he had a row—as nearly always—with the station-master, and that a man asked if he might watch us playing billiards on the hotel table; I made a break of six and he departed, obviously murmuring *Nunc dimittis*.

I am humbly but testily re-reading *Emma*. You always deride my habit of re-reading stuff to which I have been allergic, and I think it is fairly absurd. But so many good men and so many too many even better women do go on so about the woman Austen—and as Tolstoy said about lovers of Shakespeare, I can only conclude that the 'Janeites' are all mad. I am half-way through, and send you an interim report, viz that the conversations in the book fall mainly under two heads, i.e. Mrs Dale,[1] and passages to be put into Latin Prose. Mr Woodhouse ('Oh my dear, *deliciously* amusing!') hits exactly the same note every time he comes in, and the boringness of Miss Bates is positively overwhelming. No more o' that i' God's name.

Poor old Percy Lubbock is profoundly melancholy, longing to die, and ill with what sounds like dropsy (do they *tap* one for anything else?). Eupeptic women—relatives, I gather—think he should be bearing up better, as a man of philosophy and character, but the alliance of old age, illness, loneliness, and blindness is a formidable one. He is, too, a very bad patient, rebellious and wilful, and women always disapprove of that. An otherwise very sensible one was *shocked* when I quoted from a letter of Housman's how after some dinner-party, 'I ran up the stairs to my rooms, as usual, hoping to die at the top'.

[1] *Mrs Dale's Diary* was a long-running radio serial.

It may be the Indian summer of the last few days, or it may be the
H. bomb, but the fact remains that for supper this evening I had a
large plateful of big, ripe, tasty strawberries—and the three others
had large platefuls too. I hate to go on bragging like this, but I can't
get over the phenomenon myself. If we have much more of this
weather I shall have to cultivate the art of writing to you on my knee
in the garden, for this week-end it has been difficult to stay indoors.
I managed to finish the text of Oscar outside, and now there are only
my introductions to be written, and some hundred and twenty
lacunae in the notes to be filled.

Diana was indeed prompt with her invitation, and I no less with
my grateful acceptance. She said that if they weren't back from India
in time, you would entertain me. I see that Humphrey's second book
is out: have you read it?

What about the airmen who breakfasted this morning in Hong
Kong and had tea in London? My only reaction is to rush back to
Kisdon, where everything moves at a primeval pace.

Down here I now have *Many Cargoes*[1] by my bed, and read one
story a night, with much pleasure: do you remember the skipper who
loved doctoring and making a 'prognotice'? *Aurora Leigh* also keeps
going: Oscar, like you, read it as an undergraduate, but now, instead
of scourging yourself or otherwise mortifying the flesh, you force
yourself to re-read *Emma*—well, well!

By dint of talking very firmly—and very *loud*—for half an hour,
I managed to persuade the London Library committee (of which
fewer than half turned up) to endorse my plan for carrying our appeal
to the Court of Appeal. Roger, Harold Nicolson and old John Hugh-
Smith had previously agreed to oppose me, but Roger and Harold
allowed themselves to be persuaded, and no doubt Hugh-Smith
would have been too, had he not been too deaf to catch a word that
anyone said. This left him in a puzzled minority of one, wondering
what had happened to his allies. Did you see that Brendan Bracken
left £1000 to the Library? And the same to the Royal Literary Fund.

On Friday we had our half-yearly sales conference, at which for

[1] By W.W. Jacobs.

two long hours I harangued the assembled 'travellers' on the merits of the firm's autumn books. Luckily I was feeling quite brisk, and they seemed reasonably impressed. I still haven't started work on Diana Cooper's second volume, but must do soon. On Thursday Adam is coming up to London for the night. Each holidays he comes for a good dinner and a play: goodness knows what I'll take him to.

I spoke to T.S.E. on the telephone last week. He seemed pleased with his play's[1] reception in Edinburgh: packed houses and arguments between critics. It opens in London on the 25th, the eve of his seventieth birthday. On the great day itself Ruth and I are bidden to the Eliots' flat for drinks. You shall hear all about it. We saw a lot of them during the last London Library appeal, and have grown very attached to them.

I am toying with the idea of compiling (when Oscar is finally polished off) an iconography or *catalogue raisonnée* of Max's drawings. Such a thing is badly needed, since there's no way of finding out how many there are, or where. There would be no money at all in it; in fact the job would get pretty close to that 'pure scholarship' which is its own reward. And it would be essential to obtain Lady B's full co-operation and goodwill. Even now I amuse myself, between sleeping and waking, by trying to decide how such a compilation would be best arranged: chronologically would clearly be best, but as many of the drawings are undated, that presents difficulties. The ones reproduced in books or listed in exhibition-catalogues would be comparatively easy, but even then their present whereabouts would take some finding. The Ashmolean at Oxford has a fine collection— but I am drooling on, it is midnight, your patience is running out, and I have to catch the 8.45 train in the morning. So the last section of Sheet Four, must, I fear, remain unutterably blank.

17 September 1958   *Grundisburgh*

The family holidays here are just ending and P. and I return to our normal Darby and Joan existence. Last Sunday we filled three pews in the parish church, which made a considerable sensation among the

[1] *The Elder Statesman.*

worshippers. An elderly parson, known to be pretty gaga, was so staggered that he prayed for the Duke of Wales and Elizabeth the Queen Edinburgh, and later gave out that there would be no Communion service on the 58th of the month. You will enjoy grandchildren. The discovery, when they get to about eight or ten, that to them grandfather is an amiable and quite harmless old fuddy-duddy soon ceases to have any sting in it.

Did you get that thunder-plump on the very evening after you finished your letter glorifying the weather and positively swanking about your strawberries. I wish I could raise you, as they say in poker: the best example of the successful counter—stop me if I have told you—was when our Vice-Provost Warre-Cornish went to London to attend a Sotheby auction at which a copy of the Mazarin Bible was to be sold. In the bus was a fellow-librarian from Cambridge who called out with a genial sneer 'Come to bid for the M.B., I suppose?' 'No thanks', said old Cornish; 'I've got a better one at home.' Isn't the copy in the College Library actually the best or at any rate one of them? You probably know. Rather pleasant to be able to make an answer which no other man in the whole world could truthfully make. I don't know how Eton got it. Stolen, perhaps, by Nicholas Udall, the Headmaster who stole the college plate, was homosexual, went to gaol, and on coming out was made Headmaster of Westminster. Those were the days!

I have finished *Emma*. The second half is better than the first, but much of the dialogue nearly kills me with its insipidity—yet the David Cecils would see in it irony so delicate as to escape myopic eyes and coarse tastes like mine.

I saw you got your way over the London Library in spite of John Hugh-Smith's opposition. He is a rum old bird. I have known him since 1892 at prep school, and he was in Arthur Benson's house at Eton, and at Trinity. We always quarrelled, and are now bosoms, when we meet, i.e. about every five years. He was at Diana's prewedding party last year, his chest so heavily equipped with gadgets as to resemble the engine-room of a submarine; but he paid little attention to it and heard practically nothing that was said to him—or else, which is equally likely, heard it but paid no attention. He is a relative of Pamela's and greeted her with the breezy question 'Are all you girls still alive?', the youngest of the girls being over fifty. Luckily they all are alive; not that he would have turned a hair whatever the answer, which I don't think he waited for. I remember him asking Arthur Benson at Boys' Dinner 'Sir, would you take orders if you were in the running for the headmastership?' to which the reply was 'My dear John, that is the kind of question that should never be asked.' Was J.H-S. abashed? He was not.

I am glad you have resumed W.W.J., the perfect bedside literature; it must be good for any man to fall asleep gently grinning. I remember the doctoring skipper—and the patient who had paralysis but, after a dose or two of the mate's medicine, leapt out of bed, and ran up the rigging like a cat. W.W.J. has the same absolute rightness of touch in words as P.G. Wodehouse and Misses Somerville and Ross. And do you know there *are* people, I have met them, who see nothing in any of them, just as some morons, believe it or not, can't see that J. Austen is on the same level as Shakespeare.

What rot that the C. Morgan life has fallen through—though it might well have over-burdened you, but the *catalogue raisonnée* of M.B. would surely give you plenty of fun. I did not realise his drawings were so much all over the place.

I have a small literary job in prospect! Dick Routh[1] has undertaken a *small* dictionary of national biography, no doubt for the rising generation of readers who couldn't tackle the large one, and he wants me to do some of the men of letters—about 600 words each. I think it might be quite a nice little bread-and-butter job. I shan't be expected to throw new light on anyone or anything.

21 September 1958   *Bromsden Farm*

Those lists which each spring and autumn reach you looking so fresh, and occasionally tempting, are always a source of the utmost mortification. Each time I am *sure* that there will be *no* books for the next list: then at the last moment I manage to scrape together a sufficiency, but by the time I have written or rewritten those frightful 'blurbs' I am so sick of them all that I can barely stand

[1] Eton master.

hearing them mentioned. Some weeks pass, and then the finished article always surprises me by being much less awful than I remembered. And so it goes on, and goodness knows what will be in the spring list!

Tiresome though it may be, I can't resist telling you that on Friday Comfort picked *three hundred* ripe strawberries (she got so bored with it that she counted them to keep herself amused) and another basketful today: we just eat and eat and wonder.

Your job for Routh sounds rather amusing: let me know which literary blokes you have to tackle.

Adam came up to London on Thursday: I gave him an excellent dinner and took him to quite a good murder play. Next day I gave him ten shillings and told him to amuse himself. It was his first day alone in London, and he managed very well, travelling by underground, getting himself lunch and tea, visiting three museums and three newsreel cinemas!

On Friday evening I stayed up to attend the annual dinner of the book-publishers' 'travellers', where I was the guest of my London representative. The dinner itself (in the Connaught Rooms) was very good, but the proceedings lasted from 6.15 till 10.45, and there were 450 men with all the chairs and tables very close together. Two powerful singers performed and there were speeches—the chief one by Sir Vivian Fuchs. He was interesting about Antarctica, but went on a little too long. He started well, after a tumultuous welcome, by saying he felt like the man who went to have a medical examination for an insurance policy. When it was over he asked 'How am I standing, doctor?' And the doctor answered: 'I really don't know: it's a miracle.' One of the chaps at my table asked me if I knew what the Leaning Tower of Pisa said to Big Ben—'I've got the inclination if you've got the time'—which I liked very much.

Did I tell you that next Thursday I have to make a speech at the annual dinner of the Library Association at Brighton? It will mean hiring a tail coat from Moss Bros and spending the night at Brighton, where they have booked me a room at the Grand Hotel. I think I am responding to the toast of 'Literature', but nobody seems very sure. The excellent Librarian of West Sussex (who operates at Chichester) has recently taken Orders and is now also curate of Bosham (the legendary scene of Canute's experiment). Do you think that, on the analogy of the Squarson, I'd be justified in referring to him as a Librarson?

I haven't read any of the manuscripts I brought down for the week-end, and several female novelists will soon be growing restive. Diana Cooper is getting back (from Greece) to Chantilly early in October, and if I have got her next book in shape by then, I may have to go over for a day or two. You can imagine how frustrating all this is, when I am so longing to polish off Oscar: there just aren't enough hours in the day, and in London I am still getting up at 6.30.

24/25 September 1958   *Grundisburgh*

How my mouth waters at the prospect of Max's cartoons, even more than at your three hundred strawberries. How can such things be? I should like to say with conviction, as old Johnson did on one occasion: 'Sir, you must not tell this story again; you cannot think what a poor figure you make in telling it'. But somehow I find myself forced to believe it. I am interested that Comfort finds counting a palliative of boredom—because that is the only way I can get through doing four hundred strokes of the hand-pump which empties the flooded cellar. There is an electric pump, but in Suffolk whenever there is a thunderstorm all electricity is cut off and the pump doesn't work. I find the best method is to count *one* 10 times, two ditto and so on. I used to recite *Paradise Lost*, but it slowed down the pumping.

When I have finished setting papers I shall embark, six hundred words apiece, on George Herbert, Herrick, Heywood, Surrey and Hakluyt for Routh. I shall enjoy doing 'em, but I don't suppose they will be up to much.

Those dinners can be very long—songs and speeches and a comedian were the order of one devastating evening in Ipswich some years ago—the centenary of some Ipswich cricket club—from 7 to 11. The *va et vient* was incessant, but I sat solidly through the four hours to the astonishment of my leaky neighbours. It is one of my few accomplishments, but not, I fear, one that will be mentioned in my obituary, still less on my tombstone. I like Fuchs's story of the man insuring his life. I have had only one examination and had some pleasure in writing down that I had had two operations, viz cholecyst-otomy and cholecystectomy. The doctor professed astonishment, clearly underrating the pedant's penchant for outlandish Greek derivations. There is sometimes a wild beauty about scientific terms. Tennyson would have loved 'dextro-mendelic-laevomenthelesta', and anyone but a zoologist hugs himself with delight before that repulsive toad-like monstrosity at South Kensington whose name simply is *squatina, squatina, squatina*. Did you ever get far enough in maths to tackle problems about the behaviour of 'a perfectly rough insect'? Though of course, as Winston, *aetat* ten, found out, it is just as absurd that *mensa* should have a vocative.

I much regret never seeing the *Manchester Guardian*, and should be very grateful for any plums you cull from it. Is Roger in it every week? I heard from him a day or two ago. He seems in good fettle but is afraid he may not be much at the Lit. Soc. this autumn as he is 'deep in the pocket of Lord Beaverbrook', whatever that may mean. He professes to be thinking as tenderly of Chiang as Mr Gladstone did of the Bulgars; and apparently backs Mr Dulles's sabre-rattling. What odd mental pictures we have of ourselves, none surely odder than Roger seeing himself as Horatius Cocles.

I am not sure about 'Librarson'. Isn't it rather too near 'Abhorson', a name of dreadful note?[1] Some names get right into one's midriff. I always had a horror of Mr Murdstone in *David Copperfield* quite apart from what he did.

28 September 1958   *Bromsden Farm*

Once again the Gibbon quotation[2] brought down the house and redeemed my speech from total banality. I have now worked it off on the Antiquarian Booksellers and the Library Association, so don't see much chance of using it again on this side of the tomb—or the Atlantic. The Brighton affair was ineffably tedious: a mediocre and protracted dinner with insufficient liquor (during the W.C. interval

[1] The executioner in *Measure for Measure*.
[2] About the Emperor Gordian. See Vol II of these Letters, pp 94–97.

before the speeches I nipped out to the bar for an extra brandy), and five speeches (two of them by gigantic women) before mine. After having to hire a tail coat for the occasion, my mortification was completed that morning by T.S.E. (bless him) ringing up and offering me and Ruth two tickets for his first night that night. Next day (Friday) R and I attended his birthday party at 6 p.m. Only twelve people, with champagne and birthday-cake, and all his presents laid out on a table. I lit the cake and told him he must blow all the candles out with one breath, which he meekly knelt down and did. I instigated Epstein (who was nothing loth) to propose his health, and when we had all drunk it, T.S.E. said, very simply and with evident truth: 'This is the happiest birthday I've ever had.' Both Ruth and I have come to love him dearly: he is so affectionate, simple and modest, and in private his sense of humour is fine. We gave him a little old silver snuffbox and a specially bound copy (all leather and gilt edges) of the Symposium about him.

Yesterday (Saturday) I drove seventy miles to an enchanting little church at Fisherton-de-la-Mere, near Salisbury, for the memorial service to my lifetime friend Edie Nicholson (widow of the painter). It was at 3.15, and realising that Siegfried Sassoon lives only five miles away, I boldly invited myself to lunch with him. (Although we have corresponded for many years, and have numberless mutual friends, particularly E. Blunden, we had never met before.) He lives quite alone with a housekeeper in a huge and lovely Georgian house, set in a vast park, nobly timbered and surrounded by miles of wall. The spreading lawns are all long grass, except for an area next to the house. The drive is overgrown and inaccessible, so I had to leave my car by some long stables and approach the house through a shrubbery. Inside, one huge room opening into another, one after the other, all with fine books and pictures. In the hall S.S.'s bat and pads proudly displayed, for though well over seventy he still makes some runs. He is thin, tallish, good looking with a large but not noticeably Jewish nose: a tonsure-sized bald patch covered by profuse and only slightly grey hair from in front. Dressed in flannel trousers, dark blue blazer and loosish collar. Although he complained of lumbago, he rushed about speedily. He was neurotically nervous to begin with, and didn't look at me for almost an hour. He gave me a glass of sherry, said he never drank in the middle of the day, and asked whether I could manage half a bottle of claret. I said yes, and he bustled off to the cellar and returned with a half-bottle of Beycheville 1933—terrifically good—with which I washed down some fine roast duck. We talked nineteen to the dozen, about Oscar and Max (whom he knew well: he has six or seven drawings), Edmund B., Nicholson, Gosse etc. Gosse, he told me, though perfectly normal in every other way, had what can only be described as a passion for S.S.'s uncle Hamo Thornycroft, the sculptor. When someone asked Lytton Strachey whether Gosse was homosexual, L.S. said—wait for it—'No, but he's Hamo-sexual', which I thought rather good. Eventually I had to tear myself away, for fear of missing the memorial service altogether. I truly believe S.S. enjoyed the visit as much as I did—which was immensely. At any rate he begged me to return as soon as possible, for as long as possible, but goodness knows when I'll have the time. He confessed to being terribly lonely, especially in the winter.

Do let me see your potted biographies when they're done. I once asked G.M. Young how to pronounce Hakluyt. He said: 'Hacklewit, of course: it's an old Devon name'. So there!

Peter has finished his book on the Boxer Rebellion, and I shall send it to the printer this week. He flew up to Scotland the other day to shoot with Gavin Astor and the P.M. He said the air was black with grouse, and the P.M. shot well. Their best day was 160 brace. Next Tuesday I am to dine with the Priestleys—and for supper tonight I had a soup-plate piled high with fresh strawberries and cream!

1 October 1958   *Grundisburgh*

I am glad to hear the Gibbon did its customary job. Even at the M.C.C. annual dinner I had to stop while they laughed—when I was halfway through the next sentence. They see the length of a ball quicker than the point of a joke. Apropos of cricket, I was browsing in an *Ego* last night and found that C.B. Fry's order of merit over the ages was Ranji, W.G., Trumper, Bradman, Hobbs, on which I make two comments (1) How can anyone be *above* W.G. or Hobbs, or alternatively, as the lawyers say, how could either have done more than he did? and (2) Ranji and Fry always over-estimated each other, both apparently blind to the stark fact that each was found wanting in too many Test matches, which after all is *the* test of the *whole* cricketer—body, mind, and heart. C.B.F., for so clever a man, was very inaccurate; he never, e.g., remembered that Lockwood and Richardson were at their best together in very few matches, as in R's *great* years, 1895-6-7, L. was sunk in whisky, and when he revived— in 1898—R. was going downhill. But in the 1898 Surrey v Yorkshire, when Y. got out twice under 180 (my *Wisdens* are in New Zealand) on a plumb pitch George Hirst told me he 'reckoned it was the best bowling he ever had to face—no rest at either end'. Those lists in order of merit are silly; there are too many candidates. It is a case of 'there is no measuring the precedence between a louse and a flea' at the other end of the scale. But how bored you must be with all this. It is one of my bonnet's bees. Sorry.

As to the T.S.E. symposium I don't really feel that I have the shadow of a right to your generosity because, much though I liked him at the Lit. Soc. dinner, I have never been a fan, my line about his poetry always having been that of the old Scotch peasant-woman who, after praising a sermon, and being asked if she had understood it, replied 'Wad I hae the presoomption?' And the fans (like J. Austen's) irritate me when they ecstasize over the '*poetry*' of some line in e.g. *The Cocktail Party* like 'She will be coming later'. But don't let that make you think for a moment that I don't know he is a great man. The trouble is no doubt—and many must feel it besides me—that if one's tastes were mainly formed before 1914, one is bound to be, as regards modern writing, in a fine chaotic bewilderment in 1958. It was a pity too that even before 1914 the veins in all the arts were really worked out—poetry, music, painting—all were at a lowish ebb. I hope matrimony won't prevent T.S.E. coming to the Lit. Soc.

Your account of Siegfried S. is very interesting—and sad too. *Why* is he so lonely? He must have any number of friends, and is there no wife and family, and is he bereft of employment and no longer interested in the passing show? Perhaps like old Carlyle he has lost faith in both God and man—which anyone may well have done.

Gosse! Hamo!! *Pauvre humanité!* I appreciate your editorial touch, keeping the Strachey jest till one turned the page. Is *anyone* in the clear once and for all? Shall we one day have spicy hints about Mr Gladstone *vis-à-vis* Randolph Churchill? *Infandum!* But the trend in plays and novels seems almost all one way now. Last week I read *Cat on a Hot Tin Roof*. Perhaps it is better on the stage, but it is poor reading, though it fulfilled its bedtime function, viz sending me happily to sleep. When up and awake I am re-reading *Hamlet*, full of the views about him of Rebecca West and Señor Madariaga, which I doubt not you know. They completely upset the age-old view of him as a gentle weak-willed visionary. Surely the actual evidence for their view is very strong, and how does the Bradleys' and Dover Wilsons' belief in his lovableness and high-mindedness square with 'I'll lug the guts' etc? It is all very strange. I wonder old Agate didn't spot it. He would have welcomed the idea that Ophelia was no innocent.

Thank you for 'Hacklewit'. I shall certainly use it and will send you the potted life. I can't see your heartbeat quickening over it.

Yes, Roger in the Beaver's camp is very odd. Liberal principles and Tory cash, is it a case of?—with the usual result. I don't in the least know how deep his Liberal roots are; sometimes I think he regards them (and himself holding them) as a great joke, and enjoys keeping everyone guessing. The dear man, as far as I can see, affects to be pro-Chiang in the far east. I am sure that on the Judgment Day we shall find R. watching the proceedings with a gentle and apprecia-tive smile, and even then won't definitely know whether he is moved, or amused, or apprehensive or what. He is writing a Penguin about Liberalism and tells me his main trouble is to understand on Tuesday what he wrote on Monday. It must hamper progress a good deal!

By the way I did old Agate an injustice. He did see the ugly side of *Hamlet*, and complained that it was often so much cut about that it didn't emerge. I should like to have seen Irving.

5 *October 1958* *Bromsden Farm*

I completely agree about the inanity of trying to arrange cricketers of different periods in any sort of order of merit—or poets, musicians, actors or novelists either—and it is a sure sign of poverty of thought when a critic can praise one performer only by running down another. We shall never know whether Irving was a greater actor than Garrick, and who cares? Let Trumper and W.G. sleep in peace with their deathless and unclassifiable fame.

Siegfried has always been neurotic and homosexual: the first war shattered him beyond recall. In middle life he married Hester Gatty and had a son called George. The marriage held together precariously for some years, and then Hester left. Siegfried was pathologically affected by this, and for some time refused to speak to even his oldest friends unless they promised never to see or communicate with Hester again. E. Blunden for one refused to comply (he didn't particularly want to see her, but was sorry for her and refused to be dictated to). After some years S. took him back to favour. Now Hester lives in Scotland, George is a married scientist with no literary interests, and Siegfried is an ageing ghost in a huge disintegrating frame. When occasionally he stirs outside it and meets congenial people he enjoys it enormously, but for the most part his neurosis makes him play the hermit, writing occasional poetry and prose. He has always been well enough off. One of the best of his later poems was written on the birth of his son: here it is:

MEETING AND PARTING

My self reborn, I look into your eyes;
While you, unknowing, look your first time on me.
Thus will *you* stand when life within me dies,
And you, full knowing, my parting presence see.

Alone I stand before my new-born son;
Alone he lies before me, doomed to live.
Beloved, when I am dying and all is done,
Look on my face and say that you forgive.

Do get his *Collected Poems* if you haven't got them. He's a very fine poet—and crystal-clear always.

When I was a student at the Old Vic Ernest Milton played Hamlet, not perhaps according to the latest views of today, but in a frankly *sinister* way (nothing lovable or sunny about it), which seemed to fit the words very well. I always love seeing parts played in totally different ways. Sybil Thorndike played St Joan (as Shaw meant) as a bumptious North Country lass: Madame Pitoeff as a tortured mouse. This altered the whole emphasis of the play but didn't spoil it—which proves the play's worth, to my mind.

My dinner with the Priestleys was agreeable—excellent food and the great man amusingly mellow. The other guests were Leonard Russell (Literary Editor of the *Sunday Times*), his wife Dilys Powell, and a television producer called Grace Wyndham-Goldie.

On Friday I took my French novelist Maurice Druon to the Tower of London, which has a place in his next historical novel. The Resident Governor, Brigadier Wieler, to whom I had written, received us with sherry and much courtesy, and for an hour and a half we were immersed in armour, dungeons, executions and escapes. I always find the place most moving and exciting. Do you? My Frenchman adored every moment.

Alas, the strawberries are now under water, but Duff ate a plateful on October 1. Thank goodness this house is not in a valley: we've water enough as it is. Celia Fleming put all their clocks *on* an hour last night, so they have been in great confusion all today.

8 October 1958   *Grundisburgh*

That is sad news of Siegfried S.—such a good poet, I agree. 'Meeting and Parting' has real quality. And how nice it is to *under-stand* at once. It is not only the poets of our day who baffle me, but isn't a great deal of the prose also very cryptic? I mean, in the *New Statesman* review of your T.S.E. symposium, what the hell does K.E. Gransden mean in his first sentence by saying T.S.E.'s play 'seems to have divided the admirers from the Myras?' I suppose the itch to be smart and up to date is irresistible. I hate it.

According to Madariaga, Kean and Lamb were mainly responsible for the sentimental view of Hamlet, and the Bradleys and Dover Wilsons have stressed the 'lovable' note in our day. Did the Trees and Victorians generally cut out the 'I'll lug the guts' etc and muffle H's frank murder of Rosencrantz and Guildenstern and, what when once pointed out seems obvious, viz that Ophelia isn't at all shocked by the shocking things he says to her. Have you ever drawn T.S.E. on these and cognate things?

That is very interesting about *St Joan*. I only saw Sybil T. and I expect would have scouted the notion that Joan could be played differently—and even now I don't see how a 'tortured mouse' (your words) could have led the French into battle. Some critics today run down the play, for which I hope they will in the next world be particularly damned. And I see that K. Tynan not only accuses T.S.E. of sentimentality in his last play, but derides anything to do with Christianity or even religion as if it were beneath the respect of any intelligent man in 1958. But you know, this won't do. A man may have no religion himself, but if his opinions on life and literature and serious drama are to appear in print, he must show that he understands what religion has meant and means to many, or his judgements will be essentially shallow. Wasn't this the central vacuum which made many of Lytton Strachey's character-studies inadequate and even trivial? He had no idea what religion was supposed to be about. But they tell me K. Tynan is very fine. I never see the *Observer*, but even before I knew Ivor Brown I resented his being ousted to make room for a callow young smarty—who incidentally was largely responsible for boosting *Look Back in Anger*.

The Tower is a tremendous place. My ideas of it were gained from Harrison Ainsworth and I can never see it except as profoundly grim. Do you remember Macaulay's fine paragraph beginning 'There is indeed no sadder spot on earth than that little chapel' (quoted from memory—as one might say poured from a vessel full of holes)?

11 October 1958   *Bromsden Farm*

Mark the date, for this morning we removed the nets from the strawberry-beds, which are still covered with fruit and *flowers*. I write this not in vaunting vein but as a scientific Selbornian fact. A good bonfire is going in the orchard, but the B.B.C. prophesies rain, and no doubt this idiotic moon-rocket will further disturb the already chaotic atmosphere.

146

Sunday noon

For some unexplained reason I had a splitting headache all yesterday. Nevertheless I was determined to finish the proofs of Mary Lutyens's youthful autobiography,[1] and they kept me up till 1. am. I then slept for *nine* hours, and woke with my headache as before—isn't it tiresome.

You're right about the poor quality of much of today's prose: smartness is all. I imagine 'Myras' was a reference to a skit on T.S.E. called *The Sweeniad*, recently published, and written by some dim Cambridge don masquerading as 'Myra Buttle'.

Next time you catch T.S.E. at the Lit. Soc. you must tackle him on *Hamlet*. The traditional answers to your questions are (1) Ophelia was too innocent and silly to understand most of what Hamlet said to her. (2) R. and G. were spying on Hamlet and deserved to be murdered. (3) When you have just killed the wrong man by mistake, such words as 'lug the guts' might be said by anyone, and H had never respected Polonius anyhow.

Siegfried has now asked me to be one of his literary executors, along with E. Blunden and G. Keynes. Apparently he has voluminous diaries, which he thinks I'm just the chap to edit! Might be most amusing.

Peggy's play *Shadow of Heroes*[2] is terrifyingly good, gripping one all through and leaving one limp and gasping. Brilliantly produced and acted, whatever the smarties say (I have just seen the Sunday papers).

19 October 1958   *Bromsden Farm*

I'm sorry, but this pleasurable habit has overcome our neutrality pact, and in any case this won't be more than an interim scrap. I am staving off a cold or chill (which latterly I have successfully avoided), so do not feel any too bright. Also cows keep breaking into the garden, playing havoc with lawn and bed, and have to be ejected.

Tell Pamela that if her other two daughters are as beautiful and attractive as the two I've seen, I begin to understand why they have

[1] *To be Young* (1958).
[2] By Robert Ardrey, about the abortive Hungarian revolution of 1956.

147

been kept away from me all this time—I am distracted enough as it is.

Needless to say, *you* were a *succès fou* with Ruth the other evening, and she wished I had done quite a bit more telephoning!

It was nice coming on you in Foyle's, which I pass through often. If one has the patience their open shelves of secondhand books are often rewarding, since they've no idea what they've got. Nowadays most booksellers know only too well.

I have just finished the new Graham Greene ('Grim Grin' he is called in France), which I enjoyed lightly.[1] He is by now a very practised hand. I have begun Wheeler-Bennett[2] (I thought his wife charming) and there are other books piled up waiting.

If only someone would leave me a Cézanne, I would gratefully retire from publishing and London. Then your weekly letter might be longer—and even duller!

23 October 1958   *Grundisburgh*

I very nearly did the same—and regret I didn't—and wrote to you last week in spite of our compact; I ought to have known that you would. Then we should have been like Charles Lamb and his friend who agreed overnight to give up snuff, threw their boxes out of window, and met each other searching for the boxes early next morning. Sorry about that chill. Coming soon after that headache—might not Nature be saying 'Hi, push some of that pile off your plate'? Not that I know a thing about it, and regard as a fool and a bore anyone, not a doctor, who gives me medical advice, as no doubt you do too. But I don't like hearing you are not right on top of the world—the world is grim enough even when one is.

Cows—yes we have suffered from them in the same way. Not only do they muck up lawns and barriers, but nothing contents them but the best, e.g. they eat the heart out of every lettuce and leave the rest. The only silver lining is that a cow cannot help uttering a low but penetrating 'moo' of satisfaction when it finds something really toothsome, and at one time I could pick this up immediately from the

---

[1] *Our Man In Havana* (1958).

[2] *King George VI: his Life and Reign* (1958), by John W. Wheeler-Bennett.

summer-house and rushed out in time to limit the damage. Now we are encircled in barbed wire, and they have to confine their destructive activities to gnawing the bark off any tree that is clearly one of the best of its kind. Damn them—though I must say I do like milk, cream, butter and beef (less than mutton, however; are you with me here? Undercut I grant you, but not topside).

You made a bullseye with Diana, as I knew you would. She and A. agreed afterwards that it was one of their best dinner-parties. What excellent value Wheeler-Bennett is! He said in the heat of the moment that he intended to come more often to the Lit. Soc. dinners. Peter F. was *excellent* company on my left. I must say they are most enjoyable evenings and I can never thank you enough for getting me into them. And to top all there is that golden hour in your flat before the Lit. Soc. To hear that your Ruth was not bored with me goes straight to my heart and to the tips of my ears which have tingled ever since. And I thought their tingling days were over. But *I will* make a riposte to her benediction—a riposte which I suspect you may easily think intolerably impertinent, and she too, which if so you must keep it hermetically from her, and here it is—that after meeting her twice, I should quite truly and definitely have thought less highly of you if you hadn't fallen in love with her! Does that make you think me an intolerable bounder? Probably. Call up all the excuses you can, the chief one being that charm plus and intelligence plus are a very rare blend in Suffolk—or indeed in any county.

Talking of bounders, I got, after we met at Foyle's, the *Life and Adventures of Frank Harris*. It originally appeared as *Life and Loves* and was instantly banned, so I suppose, though the Elek people don't say so, that it has been expurgated. I found the book very disappointing —partly because of the boredom of the never-ending catalogue of his own achievements—invariably triumphant—and partly through a pervading suspicion that half his tales were not true. But mainly because it just isn't good enough. Few of the character-drawings seemed to me good, and few of his judgments on men and things have much weight or wit. I suppose he was before your day, but surely O.W. and M.B. and George Moore must have had a pretty clear notion that he was *the* man of four leters, if ever there was one. Or was Alfred Douglas his superior?

149

I like 'Grim-Grin'. The French always know exactly where the nail's head is. '*J'aime Berlin*' for Chamberlain when kow-towing to Hitler, and their faulting the education of the P. of W. and the late King as having 'too much Hansell (their tutor) and not enough Gretel'. Hansell, I believe, was the worthiest, and stupidest, and primmest of prep-school beaks. I remember enjoying *The Quiet American* and will get hold of this latest.

Did I tell you that I went to two horror films in London to see if their blurbs were right in promising that my hair would behave like quills upon the fretful porpentine? Alas, at one I fell asleep, and my only reaction on a close view of the faceless man was to think how nice it would be if far more people *were* faceless. I forget exactly why he was, but perhaps the fact that he was buried with Pompeii, when Vesuvius erupted, is a satisfactory explanation. I am looking out for a Cézanne for you.

26 October 1958   *Bromsden Farm*

Diana Cooper, back in England for a week, is going to ring me up tomorrow, expecting me to have got her next volume into shape—and I am only about two thirds of the way through. Since I have had the typescript for the best part of two months, always deferring it in favour of something more pressing, I now feel bad and guilty about it. The fact that Diana would never dream of blaming me only makes it worse. So I must work hard and late tonight, and in the morning train, and tomorrow night in the flat. You've no idea how the very sight of a thick bundle of typescript depresses me. Which shows that I wasn't cut out for a publisher, for your born one is forever cheerful and expectant.

In bed I have been reading with great joy Eric Linklater's new novel *Position at Noon*. It's a delightful *tour de force*, which should immediately be added to your library list. I keep thinking that if some of the young men could write half as well, they might be a good deal less angry. Let me know if you agree.

My cold was overpowering last Monday night—catarrh everywhere, all teeth aching, little sleep—but thereafter retreated, and in three days was gone, leaving me more outraged than hurt, and so many more hours behindhand with my work. Of course you're right about there being too much on my plate, but it's almost impossible to remedy, except by renouncing the plate altogether—which reminds me, I am much too fat, know by experience that I feel better mentally and physically when I'm thinner (or at any rate lighter), and shall arrange a week of starvation as soon as may be (an excellent reason for refusing all engagements). Sorry to be so self-centred.

Another cow broke into the garden, and, when pursued, cleared the fence into the field like a gazelle. Truly I hate animals, and should loathe to turn and live with them. Beef or mutton? I've never thought to compare them like that, and don't know the answer.

When I read Ruth your winged words about her she will blush with pleasure, and I shall have great difficulty in restraining her from writing you a love letter!

The only point of Frank Harris's so-called autobiography was its persistent obscenity, all of which was removed for the London edition, leaving only his lies and slipshod prose. I could have told you not to waste your money on it, but perhaps you hoped that, like the horror films, it might stand your hair on end. I can't help applauding your questing spirit, even when it leads you to sleep uncomfortably in the London Pavilion rather than peacefully at home.

This afternoon Duff drove over from Oxford, bringing a powerful friend, and between them they dug a good stretch of the kitchen garden. Duff has been put in charge of all the arrangements for the Worcester College Commem Ball next June. These include purchasing £800 worth of champagne, and I only pray that neither his thirst nor his arithmetic betrays him. I imagine he does little work.

Last week Adam wrote from Eton: 'We were taken to a film called *The Snows of Kilimanjaro*. It had nothing to do with snow or Kilimanjaro, and was j. hopeless.' So much for Hemingway!

Needless to say, Oscar's final touches are again postponed until I can cope with them, and meanwhile two new caches of letters have come to light, both small but I hope interesting: I haven't seen them yet.

Waiting to be read I have *Kitchener, Sir Charles Dilke, The Abbey Theatre, The Oxford Book of Irish Verse* and goodness knows what. I should love a year's solid reading—partly planned and partly wayward. I keep taking down unread books from my own shelves, reading a chapter or two with immense pleasure, and then having to put them back, so as to correct some infernal author's typescript. You must forgive the complaining egotism of this letter: perhaps next week will show some improvement. On All Saints Day E. Blunden will be sixty-two: I have just sent him a brief birthday note. It will be a great day when he takes his 7000 books away from Soho Square, bless him.

30 October 1958 *Grundisburgh*

Your pulse I hope has by now pretty well returned to normal, now that John XXIII sits in the seat of St Peter. I haven't really followed the vicissitudes, and am still slightly hazy about that childish business with the smoke. In fact let me be quite frank and admit that the organs of human utterance are too frail to describe my lack of interest in papal affairs. And as (to me) the only duller thing I can think of is the motor-show, you will realise that the morning paper does not detain me long just now.

Local affairs are rather pressing at the moment. Yesterday I had, as President of the Ipswich Gilbert and Sullivan Society, to welcome the Mayor and escort him to his seat to see and hear *The Gondoliers*. I am sure now that I never wish to see another G. and S. opera. To *hear* eight or ten tunes out of each, yes, but the humour is all evaporated by now out of all those songs one really knows by heart. The incurably Victorian prose dialogue is dead. Some say the tunes are too, but they are not to me, and not for another decade shall I leave off singing e.g. 'Take a pair of sparkling eyes' in my bath.

You are oddly flat about beef and mutton. Did you never know the agonising choice put before you in the pre-war Simpson's—saddle of mutton or beef steak, both perfect of their kind? I have always thought of you as one who, as Johnson put it, 'minded his belly very carefully', and you have always, thank you, told me the menu at your Lucullan banquets. But perhaps I should have spotted that you are not in a gastronomic mood from your complaint that your belly is too large—which I have never noticed. I used to be able to lose one and a half stone in a summer holiday, having what they call a very rapid metabolism, and for years now I have had practically no breakfast—except away from home when I positively revel in egg and bacon.

Then—more local stuff—this evening I have to be Question-master at a clerical brains-trust in the village hall. I have looked through the questions, and shall find it rather hard to avoid a certain ribaldry. The questions are rather like those that Man Friday put to Robinson C.—and completely stumped him. You remember? 'Does God like the Devil?' 'No, he hates him.' 'But God can do anything?' 'Yes, certainly.' 'Then why doesn't God kill the Devil?' Why indeed? I expect I shall put my foot in it by betraying that I think either the lay question or the clerical answer ridiculous. We shall see.

An *entrancing* Max Beerbohm book has arrived[1]—a lovely thing to have, bless you. Caricature now is so often merely slightly rude portraiture, but M.B. knew all about it, e.g. the A.B. Walkley with his cerebral dropsy—a critic whom I am always on the verge of finding intolerable—so cultured and dogmatic and Oxonian and Jane Austenian. But I am quite prepared to be told I am wrong.

I say these young Oxonians! We had plenty of baby-rows at C. and O. half-a-century ago, but they didn't hit the headlines. Why are rowing-men always quarrelling? Perhaps because nobody *really* knows how to row, how to teach one man to row, and *a fortiori* how to teach eight men. Tuppy once picked up a little manual of rowing in Spottiswoode's, and was delighted by the first sentence he saw, in heavy print: 'Remember the oar is put into the water with the feet.' I treasure an exhortation I once heard of Jelly Churchill's describing some movement of the hands: 'It is like passing someone a plate of hot foup (you remember his lisp). It is hot, so you want to get rid of it quickly, and it is foup, so you don't want to fpill it.' Bobby Bourne says it is an excellently vivid and apt simile for that particular movement. The towing-path at Eton was full of human nature. Marsden, his eyes on his crew, bicycling into and out of the river, wet through but making no pause in his objurgations. Brinton, furlongs distant (he couldn't bicycle), crying in the wailing tones of some sea-bird

[1] *Max's Nineties* (1958).

'Try to row well; try to row well'. I once told Havvy[1] that all coaching consisted of was to shout in a furious voice, 'Three, you're late'. After an interval while his laughter was quenched in asthma, he said 'You might well do worse. Three always *is* late'.

How boring you must be finding all this. The family was in the news yesterday. Thomas Lyttelton winning the Steeplechase once again, and Humphrey fined for speeding. I shall be in to-morrow for blasphemy. Look out for it. The last batch of Brains Trust questions has just come in; they contain 'How did Methuselah manage to live so long?' and—rather with an air of *that* will make 'em sit up—'How does the panel square the account of Creation in *Genesis* with Darwin?'

I have just begun *George VI*. Wheeler-Bennett must be an unfathomable mine of learning. One has the impression that there can be nothing more to discover. What a tiresome father George V must have been—so rigid and cross and humourless; and if Hansell knew his job the princes must have spotted quite soon that their august father did not know that 'me' is the accusative of 'I'. But perhaps Hansell didn't know it either. *Dilke* I have on my list. When I was young there was a sort of 'Oh no, we never mention him' aroma about his name, and an intriguing legend that he went to bed with two women at once. I wonder if Roy Jenkins's book throws light on this. The lady (one of the two?) in the case I gather ended as a(n) R.C. of exceptional piety. Like a boy in my house who, after many warnings, was pushed out after getting drunk in Camp, and is now in a French monastery—the apple of the Abbot's eye. Who derides the usefulness of a classical education even when it stops short at *oratio obliqua*?

Does it do anything to allay your restiveness to be told that I constantly hear your praises sung—as publisher, chairman, speaker, public-spirited citizen, *bon viveur*, biographer, conversationalist—a much more comprehensive list than in the ode to Mr Pecksniff which eulogised him as 'architect, artist, and man'. Probably, like Carlyle, when told of his fame, you will grumpily reply you would much rather have a plate of porridge.

I insist on sending my love to Ruth. Somehow I don't think it will turn her head, if you pass it on. The looking-glass doesn't lie—nor the birth-certificate.

[1] R.S. de Haviland, former Eton master.

I always particularly enjoy your items of local news, and this latest crop prompts me to confess to you (possibly not for the first time) that I have never in my life witnessed a Gilbert and Sullivan opera. Some day I suppose I must, just in case they proved to be my favourite fare. If such an opportunity arose, which would you advise me to tackle first?

If I were given that Simpsonian choice between beef and mutton, I should decide by the look of the individual joints—which must show that I am, as they now say, ambivalent in this important matter. If you insisted on an immediate and binding decision here and now, I should plump for beef as the safer bet, remembering tough and undercooked mutton from schooldays. Are you answered now?

Glad you like the Max book: I find A.B. Walkley agreeable in small doses, and have several of his books. Dear old Katie Lewis, who is eighty and daughter to the first Sir George Lewis (portrayed by Max), says she knew every one of the subjects of the cartoons, except Edward Martyn and Henry Harland, of whom she had never heard. One, as you know, was George Moore's friend and butt, the other editor of the *Yellow Book*.

I'd love to watch you coping with your Brains Trust, and all those naughty questions about Mr Darwin. But next Friday it would be your turn to laugh, for on that evening I am condemned to be the Guest of Honour at the annual gathering of the Robert Louis Stevenson Society, in some temperance building off the Tottenham Court Road. I'm told the attendance will be scanty, and mostly old ladies, but one or two will know *everything* about R.L.S., and who am I to invade their idolatry? What on earth can I say? And when find time even to think about it? Oscar's remarks on R.L.S. in the letters were few and mostly derogatory, but I might make something of O's life-long dislike of Sidney Colvin: he surely is fair game. But even those references must be looked up. Why on earth did I agree to go? It was, as Henry James said of his *T.L.S.* article, 'an insensate step'.

Which reminds me that last Wednesday, on a glorious golden-sunny autumn day, Ruth and I drove down to the Sussex home of an old friend of H.J.'s, the American actress and novelist Elizabeth

Robins. She died in 1952, aged ninety, and her lovely fifteenth-century farmhouse is now a fabulously comfortable rest-home for worn-out professional women. But in a bungalow hard by lives E.R.'s old friend and executrix, Octavia Wilberforce, a delightful retired doctor in her late sixties. She gave us a delicious fricassee of chicken and lemon sponge, and produced ten letters and two telegrams from Oscar to E.R., which she allowed us to take away and copy. She has an enormous shed stuffed with E.R.'s books, letters and papers, including letters from Henry James, Shaw, Ibsen and goodness knows who. I could have spent a fortnight there blissfully. It's a goldmine for some researcher, and I think the old lady is slightly bewildered by her responsibility, and was clearly delighted to talk to two people who knew about E.R. and her friends. She particularly took to Ruth, as who would not. Your message shall be passed on.

As for all those flattering things you report hearing about me, I would indeed prefer a plate of Swaledale porridge, but in the meantime one can't help feeling both gratified and grateful. Now I must review four detective stories and finish correcting the Havelock Ellis proofs before going to bed.

5 November 1958   *Grundisburgh*

Business before pleasure: I shall be at the Lit. Soc. Tuesday. But what a silly heading—I shall be at your Dickens door at 6. pm, expecting for the nth time that the bell-pull will come away in my hand. Don't ever get it replaced, at any rate before it perishes thus.

Gilbert and Sullivan. No, I think you were of the generation which began to turn up its nose at the operettas. Humphrey, who likes any amount of good stuff that is not jazz or modern, can't bear them; he was the first I ever heard who definitely said it'was possible for music to have *too much tune*. Moreover all the G. and S. harmonies are obvious and *vieux jeu*. In fact he looks on them as many, not wholly silly, do on those who in the twentieth century were still following the Tenny-son formula, if so it can be called. He thinks as little of my riposte that 'Take a pair of sparkling eyes' will continue to be sung in baths and never Vaughan Williams or Bartok as your modern painter does of the objection to his work that no one wants to hang it on his walls. So the eternal argument goes on, to and fro. If you ever do come across G. and S. I would recommend as your first *Iolanthe* (2) *Patience* (or even first for an Oscar Wilde expert) (3) *Mikado*. These, *me judice*, have the best tunes and G's best wit.

There was an element of comedy about the Grundisburgh Brains Trust. There were rather too many questions and a few were omitted which in my opinion and Pamela's were not of general interest or importance. I boiled one or two together and in the end only two were left out. Both had been sent in by our Rector! He rather stuffily wanted to know why, and I answered with truth and nothing but the truth that they were not on my paper, leaving him under the impression that somehow the slip on which he wrote them had gone astray. One question was why in the Communion epistle and gospel are now separated by a hymn, and the other was why do the R.C.s celebrate a different number of Sundays after Whitsun than does the C. of E. The panel had no idea that they did—and if you can think of a topic more completely empty of interest or moment I should like to hear it.

The flaw of course of all such affairs is that there are no atheists, or even agnostics, in the audience. I always hope to hear asked—Why are so many churchy people conspicuously uncharitable, censorious and narrow-minded? and How is it that, as we see so often, it is perfectly possible for a man to be upright, just, charitable, magnanimous etc without any religion at all, e.g. old Judge Holmes?

Please tell me on Tuesday *all* about your R.L.S. occasion, because I scent a bouquet of richly absurd possibilities. I hope you may have said what I have always wanted to, that I like everything about R.L.S. except his more affectionate admirers (the same feeling so many of us have about Lamb and I have too about J. Austen). And of course many of his detractors, though I suspect many of these are really objecting more to the *Schwärmerei* about him in the Nineties. Do you see that a Penguin history of Victorian Literature has come out, mainly compiled (according to the *T.L.S.*) by members of one university and five at least from one college. The quotations show pretty clearly that the articles about Arnold, Tennyson etc are by members of Downing College, damn their horrid, spiky, little dry souls. As for *that man,*[1] he should be put on a desert island with Edith Summerskill, Barbara Castle, and Beatrice Webb; that must surely be *one* of the many kinds of hell a resourceful deity has devised.

I wonder why O.W. disliked R.L.S. Too hearty perhaps. Was it he who said that he understood R.L.S. had written a book about his Travels in the Cevennes with Sidney Colvin? It sounds like him.
P.S. Will you give away the prizes at the Abbey School (girls) Malvern on June 5? It *would* be fun!

Saturday night, 8 November 1958   *Bromsden Farm*

I didn't come down here till this morning, having been delayed in London by the Robert Louis Stevenson Society. The whole evening was richly comic, and at the same time rather touching. I enclose the programme, so that you can briefly survey the full horror. It took place in two small rooms of some sort of students' club connected with London University. There were twenty-eight people present, mostly elderly ladies and old men with deaf-aids. I and the President (a nice Yorkshire novelist called Lettice Cooper) had comfortable chairs behind a table, but most of the audience were on hard wooden collapsibles. Soon after the President had begun her introductory remarks a late-coming old lady slipped in and sat on one of these, which collapsed completely, precipitating her onto the floor. She was patched up, and the fun went on. The two musicians were determined ladies of uncertain age with short grey hair. Miss Somebody, in particular, attacked the piano with gusto, as if to make sure she got full value out of each note. Never has a previous announcement of composer and piece been more necessary. The young lady from Samoa was rather beautiful in a husky Polynesian way, with long black shining pigtails, and a pink chrysanthemum over one ear. Forewarned of her approach, I greeted her with some lines of verse written by R.L.S. for an earlier Samoan beauty. My half-hour of random jaw and readings from letters (Oscar and Henry James) seemed adequate—at least they took it in silence, and no one else fell off their chair. At the end I had to ask these poor old creatures to stand for a minute in solemn silence to

[1] F.R. Leavis.

158

the Immortal Memory, after which Miss Reeves sang 'Under the wide and starry sky' rather well, and we adjourned for sausage-rolls, sandwiches, cake, coffee and fruit—all good and plentiful, but difficult to handle standing up and besieged by old ladies longing to explain their or their families' long-connection with R.L.S. Then Miss Somebody got going again, and I thought of

> The Abbé Liszt
> Hit the piano with his fist.[1]

Then Miss Reeves sang 'Home, Sweet Home', almost everyone made a speech, thanking everyone else, and I walked home exhausted. It lasted two and a half hours (outrunning the programme) and they were all as nice as could be.

Sunday noon

It is, as you know, Long Leave. Adam is home, also the Linklater boy, also Bridget. Duff and his girl are driving over from Oxford for tea, so Comfort is busy roasting and baking.

Duff seems to be rather good at the Field Game these days: anyhow he scored all the six points by which a scratch beat the School the other day! Did I tell you that he has had a short story accepted by a magazine called *Argosy*?

I can't, alas, give away your prizes on June 5. My escape to Yorkshire is delayed only by the necessity of appearing at Eton on the Fourth, and I plan to rush north on the 5th or 6th. So sorry.

I went on Thursday to the opening party for Bumpus's new bookshop, and talked to Somerset Maugham (more malicious and saurian than ever), Epstein, Arthur Ransome, H.E. Bates, Ian Fleming, Frank Swinnerton (with whom I was photographed), C.P. Snow, and a mass of publishers. E.M. Forster made quite a good little speech.

On Monday Comfort came to London for *her* half-term holiday. We dined excellently at the Garrick with my sister (oysters, roast pheasant, ice-cream) and went to T.S.E.'s play *The Elder Statesman*. I was prepared for the worst, but it bettered expectation. I don't think the old pet will ever be a dramatist, and the flat pseudo-verse in which these plays are written destroys naturalism without putting

[1] From E.C. Bentley's *Biography for Beginners* (1905).

anything practical in its place. This play is tolerably acted, and there are a few good scenes and remarks, but that's all. On Monday the stalls were more than half empty, so I fear the play's days are numbered.

My friend Michael Howard, who is Lecturer in Military History at King's College, London, has just sent me the manuscript of his long-awaited history of the Franco-Prussian War. It is enormously bulky, and he wants my detailed opinion of it, being prepared, he says, to rewrite it entirely if I so advise! God knows when I shall be able to get down to it. Just now I'm correcting the proofs of a book about W.B. Yeats and reading the manuscript of a children's book. When shall I be able either to finish Oscar or to read anything for pure pleasure?

67 Chelsea Square
London, S.W.3

13 November 1958

I hesitate to interrupt your meditations about obscenity which I see you have been in the middle of. 'Something will come of this', said Mr Tappertit, 'I hope it mayn't be human gore'.[1] That ridiculous existing law about 'those whose minds are open to such influences' has had too long a run; I am always surprised to see how respectfully lawyers and others treat it. Because all the expression I have quoted really means is 'the entire human race'. But lawyers are strange creatures. When some perfectly understandable case comes up, e.g. a man has run off with a married woman, some asinine old judge will always say that he knows the jury one and all regard the man with the utmost horror. Bilge, my dear Rupert. I didn't often attend the divorce court, but I can remember noticing the jury faintly licking their lips as they gazed at some attractive and erring lady in the witness-box. They were *not* regarding her with horror. Why, by the way is Divorce coupled with Admiralty in the law-court? I must ask Somervell that at the Lit. Soc. I remember that old bore Lord Phillimore judging a case where a barge had run into a pier, and it came up that the mate had seen, some time before, what was going

[1] *Barnaby Rudge*, chapter 4.

to happen, but had kept his mouth shut (the reason being that he was not on 'speakers' with his captain). Old P. could not understand it, and eventually asked the mate—a morose and inarticulate man— 'But, witness, could you not have said to him "You goose, you goose, can you not see that a collision is imminent"?' When several of the words were explained to the man, he grunted that no, he could not have said any such thing, and we had no difficulty in believing him. Phillimore was an ultra-refined old scholar. What was that epigram about Nature making 'a brace of Phillimores' when she wanted to make two bores, and ending 'But Nature herself would yield the ghost, if asked to make a Phillimost.' Something of that sort, but I have garbled it, like Goldsmith.

We had Agnews and Cadogans to dinner yesterday: Geoffrey Agnew most affable, but, alas, my old fag and friend Alec Cadogan! Well I suppose the diplomatic iron has entered his soul, and all conversational topics are handled as if the other participants were Gromyko and Molotov. He *is* now the man in the iron mask, and poor Pamela found him heavy going. It may not be all Gromyko's fault because the Lady Theodosia C. (straight out of Trollope) might dry up the genial current of anyone's soul. She never drew breath. I hardly heard a word she said. She heard hardly a word I said, and those she did hear she ignored. Exhausting. Literally the opposite pole as a companion to your Ruth. Joan and Philip Astley blew in for an hour at 6. She spoke with marked affection of Ruth—as indeed how should she not? Philip was up to me in 1910 when he had the looks of the young Alfred Douglas. He hasn't them now, but is a very pleasant fellow.

We lunched with the Homes (she was Elizabeth Alington) at the House of Lords. The dowager Duchess of Devonshire was of the party ('Mowcher' Cecil) one of the nicest creatures in the world. They were all very funny about the recently-made peeresses; only one apparently much addition to the oratorical strength of the House of Lords, and of one all one old peer could find to say after long contemplation was that she had a very good neck for an axe.[1]

[1] Lord Ballantrae tells me that the old peer was his uncle Patrick, eighth Earl of Glasgow, a retired captain, R.N. On the first day of the peeresses' admission he met two of them in the corridor and said 'As you may know, I

Roger came to tea—full of demure and sometimes salacious mis-
chief. As you saw at the dinner he was mainly closeted with Jo
Grimond. He tells me, with no sign of anything but amusement, that
he is in the Beaver's black books for an observation made—of all
incongruous occasions—at some Jane Austen ceremony, which an
amiable journalist dug out and sent to the B. who got chapter and
verse from Roger and then wrote to R that he found the remark 'most
offensive'. I can't remember what it was, but it was roughly on the
lines that he would as soon expect fairness in the *Daily Express* as he
would a clean shirt on a cow.

16 November 1958 *Bromsden Farm*

Pausing for a moment in my meditations on Obscenity, I must
admire your daughter's crested writing-paper. Is the bird a *Hood*ed
Crow? And why is it leaning on the admiral's anchor? Presumably to
get its second wind (*ventis secundis*), though I can't make out why this
is in the ablative plural—or isn't it? Did I ever tell you of the flustered
Coldstream guardsman who was asked by the R.S.M. what the
regimental motto was. '*Nulli secundus*, sir.' 'And what does it mean?'
'Better than nothing, sir.' He was despatched to the guardroom at
the double.

I thought you were in particularly good form last week, and only
hope I didn't appear as dim as I was feeling. Nor did matters improve
later, for on Wednesday night I was obliged to sit up playing bridge
with the Gollanczes till 1. am, and was not at my best for darling old
Rose Macaulay's memorial service on Thursday morning. There I
saw many friends, including Vita Nicolson (Sackville-West) who
scarcely ever comes to London. Harold told me he hadn't heard a
word of the excellent address (they were rather far back in the

---

fought hard to prevent the admission of ladies to the House, but now you are
here may I be among the first to welcome you?' As he passed on the ladies
heard him say to a companion in his best quarterdeck voice: 'Did you see
Lady Ravensdale? My God, what a neck for the block!' Lady Ravensdale
(Lord Curzon's eldest daughter) took this as a great compliment and was
delighted.

church) and soon after it started Vita thought Harold was going to cough and forced a cough-lozenge into his mouth. This went straight down the wrong way, so the old pet had a miserable time.

Betjeman, unusually neat in a tail-coat, read the lesson very well—from *The Wisdom of Solomon*. Can you explain the meaning of 'run to and fro like sparks among the stubble'? And is it not rather hard on the beloved dead that we should pray for light perpetual to shine on them? Russian prisons contain few worse tortures.

However, the whole service was good and fitting, though it contained rather too much unaccompanied choral singing for my taste. Outside afterwards Betjeman rather spoiled his effect by wearing a battered brown round pork-pie hat, which combined with the tail-coat to give an effect of the Crazy Gang.

Divorce in the courts is coupled not only with Admiralty, but with Probate as well. 'If Probate be the price of Admiralty, Lord God, we ha' paid in full.'[1]

Your Agnew-Cadogan party sounded a little heavy. Why on earth did they give C. the O.M.? I only wish I could come next week when you asked me, if only to tell Pamela a few jokes after her ordeal. But no—I shall go further, and most certainly fare worse.

Have you been sneaking out to any more horror films?

Which reminds me, Peter thought Cuthbert was a trifle tight at the end of dinner: is it conceivable? When I told Tommy that Cuthbert was complaining because there were no announcements, Tommy said: 'Let's announce that Cuthbert has been expelled from the club.' But I discouraged him.

Did you catch James Laver's recital of the Americans' new name for the White House? The Tomb of the Wellknown Soldier. Not bad?

Tomorrow I have to lunch with several hundred chartered accountants—can you imagine?

Our Obscenity Bill may have another chance this week, and again on November 28. Did you ever read A.P.H.'s book *The Ayes Have It*? It's a full account of all he went through before his marriage bill went through. Interesting and most relevant to our attempts today. Our leading light in the House is Roy Jenkins, who wrote the Dilke biography—a most charming and able chap.

[1] See Kipling, 'The Song of the Dead'.

Needless to say, Fred *did* ask the H.M. whether Adam could come up for our silver wedding dinner, but surprisingly enough the H.M. approved, so he will come up for the evening, and the family will be complete. Somehow my old father must be coped with: I shudder at the thought of the expense.

19 *November 1958*   *67 Chelsea Square*

Are family crests generally intelligible? The crow and anchor above seem to me on the same level of incongruity as the goat and compasses or the dog and duck. And you may well ask—Why *'ventis secundis'*. There cannot be more than one fortunate wind at a time. I like *'Nulli secundus'*, the pendant to which is perhaps *'pax in bello'* which some genius of fourteen translated 'freedom from indigestion'. Old Inge had a good collection of such howlers, and made a pretty penny out of printing extracts from his commonplace book in the *Evening Standard*. I remember a good one—not a howler—viz that the great Moltke was only seen to laugh twice in his life, once when they told him his mother-in-law was dead, and once when he heard that the Swedes regarded Stockholm as a fortress. Grim!

I share your bewilderment as to why being like sparks among the stubble should be thought the height of human felicity. But the Bible can be very odd. I remember some paper of Lytton Strachey's at Cambridge in which that humorous and slightly lavatorial mind pointed out that the promise that 'out of their bellies shall rivers of water flow' was a blessing that was not confined to the elect. The sort of joke the undergraduate loves—and the undergraduate that survives in the septuagenarian!

I have seen no more horror films, but had a good day at the Queen's Bench yesterday; the case began at 10.30 and ended at 4 and though, like almost all judges, old Hilbery deliberately mumbled, both counsel and witnesses spoke up. One old woman had run over another on a Zebra crossing and the whole crux really was—was the inability of the victim to work as well as she had caused by the accident, or by her age and rheumatic condition (she was sixty-eight). She claimed two years' salary and got a year and a half's. I was glad that only one witness said zĕbra. The judge rather pointedly said zēbra.

Cuthbert was, I think, intoxicated by the exuberance of *my* verbosity rather than by those admirable vintages. He groused a little, if you please, at there being so *much* food! What he will say, soon, at light perpetual shining upon him one trembles to think.

We go home to-morrow, fog permitting; I have a school G.B. meeting at Ipswich at 2.30. I doubt if I shall make it. We have had a good ten days with four dinner-parties. Edward Ford told us all about his tutoring of King Farouk—*not* a success, largely because H.M. was firmly convinced that he had been told to spy on him. The king was covered with scent and rings and adiposity. How would he have done as Jelly's pupil?

How did your meal with the chartered accountants go off? Did you make an easy joke about the superiority of gastronomic double entry over economic ditto? Or perhaps there were no speeches. My Old Boy begins to cast its shadow. I grow too old for the Mr Chips rôle.

23 November 1958   *Bromsden Farm*

I like to think that you can't construe *Ventis Secundis* either. My family motto, which I am pretty sure was annexed by my grandfather (he compiled an almost entirely apocryphal family history), is *Dum Spiro Spero*, which strikes me as more dogged than hopeful. What is yours?

We are full of hopes for our obscenity Bill (this is our—the committee's—third one). Much depends on whether next Friday it gets a second reading 'on the nod', i.e. without debate or division. If it does it goes to Standing Committee (how tiring it sounds) and has a good chance of getting through.

My lunch with four hundred chartered accountants was pretty good hell: most of my conversation was with a slick Old Harrovian who is apparently making a fortune by retailing refrigerated pig on the Persian Gulf. Since, he explained at some length, pig is tabu for Mahommedans, all the European troops, engineers etc were screaming for sausages, pork and bacon until he stepped in with his refrigerators. What next?

Yesterday Comfort and I drove to Oxford and lunched very agreeably with Donald Somervell in his rooms in All Souls. The only other guest was Patricia Hambleden, the nicest of women. Do you know her? Daughter of Lord Pembroke, widow of the last Lord H, Lady in Waiting to the Queen Mother. Afterwards I spent a happy hour book-hunting in Blackwell's, and then we gathered for tea in Duff's sumptuous rooms in Worcester. A boil on his arm had prevented his playing rugger, and he regaled us with cream buns and other fanciful cakes. At five we went to the first house of Celia Johnson's new play, which is on its way to London—an agreeable light comedy which we all enjoyed.

To-day we planted a hundred daffodils and narcissi in the orchard, in the distant hope that Spring will one day return. The myth of Prosperine must surely have originated in one of these northern fog-bound lands, and not in the perpetual sunshine of Greece.

The family dinner-party for our silver wedding on Tuesday is beginning to loom portentously. My old father is equal to at least four wet blankets, and now Comfort has invited her mother, with whom I am barely on speaking terms, to come for a preliminary drink. Why did I ever suggest it? Why was I ever married at all?

Also I have just realised that I have failed to book a luncheon-table anywhere for St Andrew's Day next Saturday. Patricia Hambleden is taking her boy to lunch at London Airport, and if all else fails I dare say I shall do the same. My true motto is: 'If it isn't one thing, it's another!'.

This evening I heard on the radio of a teddy boy who went to a barber's. 'Short back and sides?' asked the barber. 'No', said the teddy boy; 'just change the oil.'

I went last week to a literary cocktail party at John Lehmann's. I abominate such gatherings, but couldn't get out of this one, and it was better than most: champagne to drink and just enough room to move. My old friend William Plomer told me he is writing the libretto for Benjamin Britten's new opera—all about a tortured boy in mediaeval Japan. Anywhere for a lark, I suppose.

Ruth was quite unhappy at your being so long in London without her seeing more of you, but I told her you were fully occupied with horror films and dinner-parties.

The shadow of my old boy dinner (next Wednesday) is deepening. I always dislike it in prospect and like it in retrospect—one of those anfractuosities of the human mind I suppose. Our family crest is a Moor's head and the motto is *'Ung Dieu, ung Roy'*, *ung* being, they tell me, old French for *'un'*. The resources of the English language are inadequate to depict the entire irrelevance of both. My great-great-grandfather was Governor of Jamaica; I had a great uncle who was very possibly eaten by cannibals. I know of no other connection with the colour-bar. As for the motto, it is a fine defiant gesture to nothing in particular, like many another: isn't yours a shout from some heroic last ditch? It has more blood in it than ours, and has also that pleasant English trait which Chesterton noted as part of Joe Chamberlain's appeal, i.e. the impression of a superb rearguard fight against enormous odds, when he really had all the big battalions behind him.

Talking of Joe C. I am immersed in the strange Dilke story—surely one of the oddest ever. To begin with, was there ever a drabber, duller-looking Don Juan in the whole history of romance? And what a mask those great beards were. The eyes need the mouth to complete an expression, and one can't see what Tennyson, Browning, Morris, Doughty, Tolstoy etc were *really* like. Though one knows that when Browning did shave his off, Mrs B. exclaimed 'It must be grown again this minute'. And I think it was FitzGerald who somewhere found fault with Tennyson's mouth. Dilke's face is as blank as a London fog, and I put it to you that a man who wanted—and got—*two* women in his bed must have had a fine extravagance in his make-up, and surely showed it in his face if anyone had ever been allowed to see more of it. I haven't really got to Mrs Crawford yet, who apparently ended as a saint, but never said another word about D.

Tell me all about your family party. My interest is not wholly benevolent, because from what you have let drop I scent amusing possibilities with a touch of *contretemps* about them. 'Why was I ever married at all?' is a question that I suspect all husbands have at times asked, and the question is not always rhetorical, just as Chesterton said that every thoughtful man has at one time or another thought of suicide. C.M. Wells, that whimsical man, used to maintain that the only thing that stopped him from seriously contemplating it was the difficulty of disposing of his corpse, and the awful bore it would be to those who found it. That difficulty keeps murders down to some extent (one Deeming solved it for a good many years, by burying wife after wife in his cement kitchen floor. Monty James, who had a macabre strain in his humour, used to say D's motto must have been 'Marry in haste, and cement at leisure').

30 *November 1958*   *Bromsden Farm*

I shall think of you on Wednesday, wishing I was one of your Old Boys. I always enjoyed our dinners, at which my Uncle Duff was easily the best speaker, but they died with dear old Jelly. *Ung Dieu, Ung Roy*, you know.

Yesterday was our most painless St Andrew's Day so far. Having no need to wade through mud and fog to those infinitely tedious games, we picked Adam up and took him straight to London Airport, where (amid a mass of Etonians and parents) we had an excellent lunch. The restaurant has one glass side, through which as one eats one can watch Viscounts loading and taking off for all parts of Europe. After that, with the utmost scuggery, we sat in a nice warm cinema in Slough (poorish films) until it was time for Lock-Up and tea in Adam's room. The poor child is in the middle of his G.C.E., for which he has to do *nineteen* papers. I wonder if his English ones will fall to you—or do they keep you off the Etonians, judging you no better than an Australian umpire? Certainly if I had to mark W.S. Maugham's last book I shouldn't give it more than half-marks for style and English. Those drab, broken-backed sentences (with so little behind them) might have been written by a foreign governess who had learned English entirely from books. Clearly W.S.M. has absolutely *no* ear for prose-rhythms, and very little eye, for much of it *looks* so awful. However, he's eighty-three, and a G.O.M., and he has asked me to lunch at the Dorchester next Thursday, so mum's the word.

As you say, Dilke proves—if proof were needed—that Don Juan and Adonis are two quite different people. Perhaps one could write an

168

essay showing that the greatest womanisers have always been ugly—
Casanova certainly was, but Byron must have been handsome before
he got too fat (doubtless his lameness was a great attraction).

The silver wedding party went off much better than I had expected. Preliminary glasses of champagne were drunk in the Lit. Soc.'s
sherry-room. Apart from the family (ten strong), Peter, my mother-
in-law, her semi-paralysed son, and the Hamish Hamiltons looked in.
My father tottered in for dinner, and by putting the girls (Comfort,
Bridget and my two nieces) beside him in relays, I managed to keep
him in good humour throughout. We ate smoked salmon, roast
pheasant and ice-meringue with hot chestnut sauce. The same wines
that satisfy the Lit. Soc. My brother-in-law proposed our health
graciously, and the bill came to more than £30.

Luckily next day I earned £21 by speaking for forty minutes to
some seventy members of the Book Society. A rambling jaw went
down quite well, but in the ensuing conversazione (with drinks) I was
relentlessly pursued by a coal-black, soft-spoken Nigerian, who
threatens to send me a mass of his short stories.

The silver wedding celebration made my darling Ruth very unhappy. Although it had no significance, and changed nothing, it's
easy to see how the reaffirmation of the tie that prevents my marrying
her upset her. I think she's all right now, but her misery made me feel
miserable too. As I have quoted before, 'He who lives more lives than
one . . .'

3 Wyndham House
Sloane Square

4 December 1958

As always, I enjoyed the Old Boy Dinner last night. They were
very welcoming, and all looked to me very much as they did in
Remove, what they had lost in hair being made up in waist. One—
now was it Geoffrey Davson, i.e. Anthony Glyn?—said he knew you,
and did he say you or maybe only Heinemann's were moving to new
premises? Can I face ringing a bell that does *not* come out in my hand?
I dislike old things changing.

Yes, Casanova, John Wilkes, H.G. Wells—all ugly men. George
Moore? but how far *was* he a Don Juan, for didn't some lady say he

was one who 'told but didn't kiss'? A few of the Byron pictures hint at charm, which all said was overwhelming, and he said himself that it was always the women who made the first advances to him and not *vice versa*. Who knows the truth? It will be most annoying if after all there isn't a next world where we may get the answers to all such problems—the *Marie Celeste*, Bacon and Shakespeare, the Wallace murder, the Baccarat case etc.

Your silver wedding party was a tremendous affair, though I don't *like* to think of that £30 gone west, even though much came quickly back from the Book Society; still I expect you gave a lot of pleasure.

Poor Ruth. How invincibly vulnerable is deep love. That Wilde stanza you quote is always persistently relevant—and there are those, e.g. the old Wykehamist Wavell, who said the *Ballad* was 'insincere'! We must remember that a common Wykehamist trait is to suspect the sincerity of all non-Wykehamists.

7 December 1958 *Bromsden Farm*

This afternoon I interrupted my labours on Diana's proofs to spend three solid hours going through Peter's with him, so you will understand if my usual epistolary waffle degenerates into proof-corrector's symbols. So many thousands of hours have I spent on such thankless work that I can scarcely read *any* book without whipping out my pencil and marking the solecisms, tautologies and plain errors.

Had I applied this treatment to Somerset Maugham's latest, the margins would have been black with glosses. However, at luncheon on Thursday he was at his mellowest. He hates women, and their presence always brings out his adder's tongue: on Thursday there was nobody except himself, his male secretary, John Sparrow and myself. He always has the same suite at the Dorchester on the fourth floor, overlooking the park, and the huge sitting-room is furnished with his own books, pictures, Epstein's bust of him, etc—all of which the hotel stores when he is away. Luncheon is served there by a bevy of waiters. We had Martinis, a sort of Scotch egg cooked with cheese, a tremendously good and authentic mixed grill, fresh peaches and ice-cream, washed down by copious Hock, with brandy and coffee to follow. All excellent, and of course I never stopped talking. W.S.M.'s stammer is as bad as ever, but now when he can't get the word out he snaps his fingers in a tiresome way, which he never used to do. When he first met Sparrow (not very long ago) he believed that everyone called him Johnny—and he still does, though no one else ever has. I almost did too, to keep him company. (When I was twenty, my father had a dotty old chauffeur who always called me and my sister Mr Rudolph and Miss Dreary—her name is Deirdre. We missed the moment for putting him right, and all the rest of the time he was with us we called each other by these names in his presence, to reassure him.) T.S.E. and his wife had visited W.S.M., who commented with pleasure on their evident happiness. Usually it is unhappiness and other negative states that he stresses, so I took this as a sign of grace. W.S.M. said that when he booked a passage to Yokohama for October 1959, the people gave him a look as much as to say 'Poor old josser, he'll be dead long before then.' He was wearing a purple-and-black smoking jacket, which he said belonged to his secretary. He is clearly determined to outlive Winston: what a job the obituary-editors will have if they die on the same day!

Write to Soho Square this week, if possible, so that your letter reaches me on Friday morning, when I set off in luxury (first all the way) for Chantilly. I'll write to you from there, and post it when I get back to London on Monday evening, so it may be later than usual at Grundisburgh.

The Lit. Soc. will be pale and quiet without you. Lockhart looms, but as I shall have come almost straight from Twickenham, we can talk about rugger, in which he is interested. Ruth and I have been to every University Match since 1947, and always enjoy this annual treat, whatever the game is like.

It probably was Davson (Glyn) who said he knew me. Heinemann's are indeed moving—to a new, inadequate and traffic-blocked house in the heart of Mayfair, but I hope to answer your ineffectual bell-pulling in Soho Square for the next thirteen years. Then my lease runs out, and I shall, God willing, write to you from some snug retreat in the North Riding.

The American hospitals are too good: they always get Dulles better.

You are in Henry James's predicament—who, whenever he read a novel by another, rewrote it in his mind throughout. I do the same with many a sermon I hear—generally in the way of supplying an obvious and relevant quotation. Clerical ignorance of literature seems very common now. Our man here—he came only eight months ago—goes to another extreme. Last Sunday he referred to Karl Barth and the Orphic myth, without any explanation of either. Meanwhile half the unmarried young women are with child, and many of the marriages precede or follow the arrival of the firstborn by a matter of a few weeks or even days. Not necessarily as a sequel to the Orphic myth, as none of them comes to church. And after all East Anglia has always been noted for the trial trip before marriage, as in old days husbands, especially farmers, liked to know they would have families before committing themselves.

I stayed a night recently with S.C. Roberts at Cambridge, who showed me a copy of Raleigh's *Six Essays on Johnson* that had belonged to Max Beerbohm. Some pencillings of his (very few beyond markings) were in it. He put more than one query opposite R's saying J. did not fear death, only Boswell on death, and to J's remark that 'Great people do not like to have their mouths stopped' M.B. had added 'especially by a man with his mouth full'. (Who by the way is J.G. Cozzens who, according to Colin Wilson in a monthly magazine, is 'in every way a much greater writer than Max Beerbohm'? 'In every way' is surely a little excessive.)

Pamela says the 27th will do very nicely for our annual luncheon—always one of the lights in the darkness of the dead vast in middle of the winter. Exam-papers have been coming in a steady dribble. I am just finishing the Shakespeare papers. And I declare to you, Rupert Hart-Davis, that *except for some of the poetry* greater drivel than *The Merchant of Venice* has rarely been written. I mean all the *gup* about its drama and characterisation etc. I feel sure S. meant Shylock to be a figure of hatred and derision, and was so bad a dramatist that he just didn't see that to make all the men-Christians sh-ts, and Jessica a heartless little bitch, and to give Shylock a gift of magnificent speech simply didn't make sense, but was bound to arouse admiration and sympathy. I don't believe he cared twopence about his plots or characters; he *did* care about words, and had the most overwhelming command of them that ever was. And now tell me I am an ass and simply don't understand. But when I retort that Tolstoy and I see eye to eye in this, what do you say then? That we are both asses? Perhaps you are right.

I am glad about Soho Square—though at eighty-eight shall I be able to make your stairs? Your lease will still have a few months to run. Never have a lift. Don't have that jagged tooth under your stair-rail removed or that hidden step on the top flight made visible, I *like* these things. And when I arrive panting and—only temporarily —speechless, let me always find you and Ruth *exactly* the same as ever. I may die there, as Housman always hoped to after scaling the stairs to his rooms in Whewell's Court. I *should* like that, but it might bore you.

Château de St Firmin
Vineuil
Oise

14 December 1958

Your letter arrived just as I was leaving for Victoria, and I enjoyed it in the train to Dover. My journey was enjoyably uneventful. Over the usual delicious lunch on the French train (hors d'oeuvres, fish, steak, cheese, sweet, half a bottle of Meursault, coffee and a liqueur) I chummed up to a limited extent with a pale-faced chap who turned out to be Peter Smithers, Conservative M.P. for Winchester. Then, back in my carriage, I was relentlessly talked to by a ravaged-looking female American television operative, and by the time I had moved my watch on an hour for French time we were at the Gare du Nord, where Diana was waiting with the car. Since then I have stirred out of the house only once—for a brief shopping expedition to Chantilly. Otherwise it has been sessions of proof-correction punctuated by huge and delicious meals. The cook (an English pansy, heavily made up) has been ill in bed, and *all* the work of the house has been done by a splendid Italian girl called Lucia. No one here but Diana and her secretary Norah, who was Duff's secretary. This afternoon Cynthia

Jebb, wife of Sir Gladwyn, drove out from Paris to talk about a carpet. Tomorrow I leave Paris at mid-day by the Golden Arrow. I find it refreshing to spend even a few days among quite different scenes, sounds, tastes and smells.

You ask about J. G. Cozzens. He is a pretentious American novelist of extreme volubility. His latest tome (*By Love Possessed*) has been widely acclaimed as the 'Great American Novel', so long awaited. Like those endlessly ponderous novels by Theodore Dreiser, *B.L.P.* consists of long discourses on business, sociology etc, interspersed with lubricious sex-scenes, to keep the reader going. You have been warned! Mr Cozzens is not worthy to sharpen Max's pencils.

I assure you, my dear George, that to a man who once spent several weeks holding a spear (pike or halberd) at the back of the stage on which *The Merchant of Venice* was regularly performed—to such a wretch you need say nothing of the play's shortcomings. Those interminable casket scenes—oh heaven! I'm sure you're right, and Shylock took control of his creator. I hate to agree with you *and* Tolstoy, but for once I must.

Last Monday Ruth and I journeyed to Stratford-atte-Bow (no distance on the underground: only three stops after Liverpool Street) and there paid our first visit to the Theatre Royal. It is an exquisite eighteenth-century theatre, quite unspoilt: even the bar is contemporary. The play was *The Hostage* by Brendan Behan, the Borstal boy —an extremely amusing charade with songs and tragic interludes, set in a Dublin tenement and impossible to describe. Very Irish, very fast, very gay. Some good jokes: 'What is an Anglo-Irishman?' 'A Protestant with a horse'. We enjoyed it no end.

On Thursday I lunched with Mrs Ian Fleming (née Charteris, then Lady O'Neill, then Lady Rothermere, now Mrs F). She has long been a close friend of Mr Gaitskell, and at luncheon were two of his henchman—Tom Driberg and Woodrow Wyatt. To balance them were Lady Violet Bonham-Carter (in splendid form after her world tour) and the Austrian Ambassador, who was grateful at being remembered ('No one ever recognises me'). I was between Lady Glenconner and Elizabeth Montagu, both charming. Excellent food and drink: why can I have been asked?

Next week will be much occupied with the presentation of the

Duff Cooper prize to Betjeman by Princess Margaret. You shall hear about it next Sunday. And on Tuesday an American friend is taking me to the new musical, *West Side Story*. How I do gad about! And how I'd love to get away from it all. It's usually people in the whirlpool who hate missing things: people who are happily occupied elsewhere just don't bother. Or is that wishful thinking? Anyhow it's difficult enough to arrange one's own life without trying to advise others. Now it's time for another smashing meal, and then more proofs. I shall post this on the white cliffs of Dover.

18 December 1958   *Grundisburgh*

How good you are on J.G. Cozzens. I remember now I saw reviews of that portentous book, and resolved comfortably that I need not read it. I suppose all America is lapping it up. And I get a clear little vignette of you in France. You must by now be a fully-equipped gourmet, and I follow your banquets with watering mouth. Were you, in fairly early youth, allowed to choose your favourite dishes on your birthday? A good old Victorian habit. How loftily you will smile on hearing that my choice was mince and egg and what is called summer pudding—bread soaked in some kind of fruit-juice, with of course lashings of cream. One day they sent up custard instead of cream; I never thought the same of grown-ups for years afterwards, and doubt if I don't still feel the same now (we had mince and egg and rice-pudding at lunch today—both first-rate!).

Yes, you *do* gad about. I often wish I had half your complaint, but I don't know. I should get exhausted long before you do. Fancy those innocent Yanks having in their charter 'the pursuit of happiness' as one of man's legitimate aims. Don't he wish he may get it! And who ever has? (Small point—I hope you *always* alter '*Whatever* do you mean?' to '*What ever* do you mean?' *Quodcunque* is not an interrogative.)

Bridget and Adam will be here to welcome you, but I think Duff will be away. Adam won the Junior Chess Cup at Eton: he says it's the size of an egg-cup, but I say a cup's a cup for a' that. Perhaps next year he'll win the School cup, which I believe is one of the biggest in the school. We shan't, I gather, know about his G.C.E. for some weeks.

I ate so much in France (3 lbs gain in weight) that I strong-mindedly resolved to eschew the smashing lunch on the return train —only to discover at the Gare du Nord that my seat was in the Pullman to which lunch is brought, so of course I succumbed and ate my way deliciously through hors d'oeuvres, a whole fried sole, superb veal, *petit suisse*, ice and coffee, washed down by a half-bottle of excellent wine. A brandy-and-soda on the boat, followed by tea on the English train, kept me going to London. Next day I was taken by an American friend to the terrific new musical, *West Side Story*. It is *Romeo and Juliet* transposed to juvenile delinquents in New York, and the music is loud enough to blow one's head open. The dancing is superb, and the whole thing most effective. We were in the sixth row of the stalls, and next to us was a party containing the P.M. and the U.S. Ambassador, with their wives. When the P.M. came back to his seat after the interval, the whole house cheered him. He was clearly delighted.

On Thursday, after much fuss and many arrangements, the Duff Cooper Prize was presented to Betjeman by Princess Margaret, to whom I completely lost my heart. My dear George, she is exquisitely beautiful, very small and neat and shapely, with a lovely skin and staggering blue eyes. I shook hands with her coming and going, and couldn't take my eyes off her in between. All her photographs belie her. Much champagne was drunk, and Diana was pleased.

There was *no* irony in my remark about the Lit. Soc. Martin Charteris's charming wife, whom I met for the first time the other day, said she always looks forward to the Lit. Soc. dinners, both because Martin enjoys them so, and because he retails to her all the jokes and sayings (whose? must be yours!) afterwards.

My Christmas shopping looks like being left till Christmas Eve, as usual. How cumulatively tiresome it all is. I already have almost three hundred cards.

I expect you noticed that the Government, terrified of losing East Harrow because of A.P.H.'s intervention there, gave time last week for a debate on Obscenity. Our fear now is that by the time they have finished with our Bill it will be emasculated beyond usefulness, but we still hope. The situation is complicated by the imminent publication here of a book called *Lolita*, which is clearly indecent. Although many hope that its publisher (Weidenfeld) will go to gaol, we don't want to argue our Bill under this shadow.

(University Arms Hotel, Cambridge)

31 December 1958   *Angelo's, Eton College, Windsor*

I hope you did not think our visit ended rather curtly on Saturday. But with that conjugal sixth sense that even the most unimaginative can acquire (though many don't) I could see that Pamela was fighting an uphill battle against a germ of short-lived but active malignity, which has decimated Eton since Boxing Day; and in fact she did go straight to bed as soon as she got home and missed the evening at Rose's, where Humphrey was (and it tests the utmost efforts of any germ to make her do that). All the sufferers in several different families here are comically insistent that Xmas diet had nothing whatever to do with it, but of course they convince nobody (like the Chinese proverb 'A man with a red nose *may* not drink, but nobody believes it'). It is just one of those things. She would have loved to prolong our visit to you *quam diutissime*, and so would I.

I saw a good deal about *Lolita* in the Sunday papers. When will its fate be decided? I am not sure if I wholly trust Bob Boothby's judgement on pornography, but perhaps he sways many votes. Still, if Boswell's *London Journal* passed muster, it is hard to see where the line is to be drawn.

Do you know Robert Graves? I know nothing of his poetry, but always find his prose second-rate. In his last bookmaking he records a broadcast pulling to bits Milton's 'L'Allegro'. It appears his daughter aged thirteen asked him if it wasn't 'rather confused'. He read it and in the face of scores of better men down the centuries he corroborates his daughter's opinion. A silly man, surely? There are too many about.

I found still going strong the man at Jefferies (now Thomas) who first cut my hair thirty-nine years ago. But my world thins. I told him I intended to call on Mr X. 'Oh he died three weeks ago.' 'Oh dear, then I shall go and see Mr Y.' 'He is being buried this afternoon.' Grim.

N.B. *All* the six great frosts since 1908 have begun round about Jan 20. *Verb. sap.* We leave here on the 9th, i.e. the day of the great snowfall of 1959.

INDEX

181

Thorndike, Sybil, 145, 146
Thornycroft, Hamo, 141, 142
Tim, *see* Nugent
Time and Tide, 24, 25, 26, 30, 47, 103
Tolstoy, Leo, 132, 167, 173, 174
Tommy, *see* Lascelles
Toynbee, Arnold, 44
Traherne, Thomas, 18
Trevelyan, G.M., 115
Trollope, Anthony, 28
Trott, Albert, 106
Truman, Harry, 57, 58
Trumper, Victor, 15, 68, 141, 144
Tuppy, *see* Headlam
Tynan, Ken, 71, 146

Udall, Nicholas, 135
Ulysses, 78
Upjohn, Mr Justice, 10

Van Oss, Oliver, 62
Vansittart, Lord, 88, 91
Vaughan, E.L. (Toddy), 11
Vaughan, Mrs, 49
Vaughan Williams, R., 156
Verney, John, 17, 19, 21, 24, 39
Verrall, A.W., 95
Visiak, E.H., 2

Walkley, A.B., 153, 155
Walpole, Horace, 25
Walpole, Hugh, 32, 42, 53, 55–56, 61, 104, 107, 111, 118
Ward, Mrs Humphry, 69
Warner, P.F. (Plum), 25
Warre-Cornish, F., 135
Warre-Cornish, Mrs, 94
Wass, Tom, 106
Watts-Dunton, T., 65–66

Wavell, A.P., 170
Webb, Beatrice, 32, 45, 158
Wedgwood, Veronica, 103
Weidenfeld, George, 177
Welldon, Dean, 18
Wellington, Duke of, 77
Wells, C.M., 18, 25, 34, 44, 106, 167–168
Wells, H.G., 8, 27, 28, 30, 31, 32, 35, 42, 47, 169
West, Anthony, 42, 43
West, Rebecca, 28, 52, 73, 143
Westminster, Loelia Duchess of, 16
Wheeler-Bennett, J.W., 148, 149, 154
Whitney, John Hay, 37, 176
Whitworth, Rex, 114
Whymper, Edward, 81
Wickham, A.K., 14
Wieler, Brigadier L.F.E., 145
Wigwam, Dr Virgil, 32
Wilberforce, Octavia, 156
Wilde, Oscar, *passim*
Wilkes, John, 169
Williams, Harold, 40
Williams, Mrs, 7
Williams, Sir William, 83
Wills, Mr Justice, 95
Wilson, Colin, 27, 172
Wilson, J. Dover, 143, 145
Wise, T.J., 37
Wodehouse, P.G., 52, 136
Wood, Henry, 3
Woodruff, Douglas, 23
Woolf, Virginia, 32, 105
Wordsworth, 8, 21, 35, 53, 124
Wyatt, Woodrow, 174
Wyndham-Goldie, Grace, 145

Yeats, W.B., 59, 71, 101, 115, 160
Young, G.M., 44, 141